FOR WHAT DO WE FIGHT?

NORMAN ANGELL

FOR WHAT DO WE FIGHT?

HARPER & BROTHERS PUBLISHERS

NEW YORK   LONDON

CONTENTS

FOR WHAT DO WE FIGHT?

CHAPTER I

WHAT THIS BOOK TRIES TO DO

THE chief points discussed in this book are these:

(1) The principle on behalf of which Britain and France have declared war is in truth the fundamental principle of all organized society and of orderly civilization, though not one heretofore applied to international life, nor one which has been applied in the foreign policy of Britain and France since the last war, a fact which, more than any other, accounts for our present peril. The principle they now defend is the basis not merely of social, political and economic security, but the necessary condition of those activities which give value to life; which the eighteenth-century Enlightenment defined as the Rights of Man, and which we had too readily assumed had been conquered, in the West at least, for all time. Those rights are now challenged in a great Counter-Revolution, and must be again defended or be again submerged; the centuries of struggle against the Divine Right of Kings has now been followed by the mass acceptance, over large parts of Europe, of the Divine Right of Dictators, imposing a rule more ferocious and evil than that

of the kings they replaced. Our defeat or submission would mark the triumph of that Counter-Revolution.

(2) The emergence of this form of nationalist dictatorship is very largely due to the failure of the European nations to create an international society which would ensure, by its collective power, the security of each member. Collective defence not having been realized, dynamic nations have been led to rely each upon its own individual power, thus precipitating competition for strategic frontiers irrespective of the desires of minorities, competition for self-sufficiency and for power preponderance. "Germany must dominate her neighbours as the only alternative to being dominated by them." The worship of force and violence thus becomes justified on grounds of national self-preservation. To give the State power to defend itself, individual freedom is sacrificed. This increasing subservience of the individual to the State must go on so long as each nation's security is based upon its own power, and not upon the collective power of the international community sustaining a constitution or law affording protection to each member. The price of the international anarchy is the increasing surrender by men of painfully acquired rights and freedoms. The continuance of actual or latent war between nations

must make the maintenance of democracy impossible.

(3) This relationship between the preservation of individual freedom, and the creation of an international society has never been adequately realized by the democracies. Again and again since the last war Britain and France have refused to accept the same risks for the defence of the international order which they would readily have accepted to repel attack upon their own territorial possessions, a scale of values which must make law, and ultimately defence, impossible. We have therefore our share of responsibility for the Nazi phenomenon.

(4) Our cause can triumph and a repetition of the tragedy of 1918—an immensely costly victory so undone in a few years that it has now to be fought all over again—can be avoided only if we can persuade the neutral world and ultimately the enemy people that the principle for which we now fight will be a permanent feature of our future policy; that in future our power will be used to resist aggression by the defence of its victim even though the aggression is not aimed directly at ourselves. Only by being clear ourselves on that point can we make it clear to the neutral—or quasi-neutral—world, and so render it favourable to us rather than to the enemy, deter neutrals or quasi-neutrals from being drawn or forced into policies

which economically or strategically or militarily will favour the enemy rather than ourselves. In making their choice, neutrals will have to judge whether their security after our next victory is likely to be such as will justify them in taking the risk of standing up to Totalitarian pressure, or whether it might not be better from their point of view to come to terms with Totalitarianism before sharing the fate which Czecho-Slovakia and Poland and certain other of our allies have had to face since our last victory. The judgment which neutral and enemy peoples form of our future conduct will determine their present conduct. What we stand for in the war may well determine (both by the degree of enemy resistance and the course of neutral—particularly American—behaviour) whether we shall win the war.

(5) We cannot, and ought not to state our peace terms in the sense of indicating what the future frontiers of, (say), Poland, or Czecho-Slovakia, or the future relationship of Austria to the Reich are to be. But we can, and should indicate the nature of that "new international order," of which both the Premier and the Foreign Secretary have spoken. We can do this best, and give earnest of our sincerity by *acts*; by initiating the federal unity of Europe in so developing our own relations with France as to bring about a virtual Franco-British Federal Union; and by throwing

our Empire open to the world on equal terms with ourselves *now*, by offering to give neutrals (e.g. Denmark, Norway, Holland, Belgium), the same economic position in the Empire as that occupied by the Dominions. This would be the best answer to the charge that we (Britain and the other Dominions) are waging war to retain imperialist monopolies, excluding others from "living space."

(6) If stalemate on the West continues, it can be turned to our advantage by building behind the defences of the French Maginot Line and British command of the sea, this nucleus of western unity, a nucleus which would be of strongly attractive power to the neutrals by reason of the economic advantages and political securities it can offer them. It would be calculated also to stimulate the right kind of revolution in Germany, and to meet the peculiar conditions created by the rising power of Russia. Whether this Western unification (which alone can meet the challenge of Russo-German Totalitarianism), comes into being, will depend, less upon the precise form of any constitution that may be drafted, than upon the degree of public wisdom that can be applied to its working; whether repetition of the old errors can be avoided.

(7) Bitter experience proves that certain errors and fallacies bearing on international relations persist obstinately in the public mind, influencing

elections, particularly at such times as peace settlements after war, and often paralysing the best intentions of statesmen. No "peace plan," League or Federal Union, can possibly work or even get a fair trial so long as these popular errors and fallacies persist. The history of America's repudiation of President Wilson's plans of British and French attitude towards (e.g.) Reparations at the close of the last war, illustrates the point. An immense amount of expert and disinterested labour in preparing at the close of the last war a relatively good peace was utterly frustrated by popular passion, played upon by political and newspaper demagogues; passions rooted in misconception—misconception usually of very elementary social principles. This book, therefore, does not discuss in much technical detail this or that proposed constitution, but attempts to expose fallacies and misconceptions which would make any plan unworkable. Thus also some emphasis on the nature of past mistakes.

Repetition of past errors of policy cannot possibly be avoided if we refuse to examine those errors, decline to make any real effort to discover why the good intentions of the past have been frustrated.

(8) We need to know how the principle for which we fight can be applied in our relations with Russia, Italy and Japan; to know whether, in addi-

tion to being on our side a war against Hitlerism
and Nazism, it is also a war against Bolshevism,
or whether we could with justice and safety accept
(as to within a week or two of the outbreak of
war we were ready to accept), the alliance of
Stalin against Hitler; whether the war is economic
in the sense of being resistance by a bourgeois
West to a more socialist East, represented respectively by the National Socialism of Germany, and
the Communism of Russia, or whether the territorial expansion of Russia may not be a means of
the spread of Communist revolt, which was an
early part of Soviet policy, an extension, first into
the border states and Balkans, and ultimately into
Germany itself; whether, having destroyed Hitlerism, we may find Stalinism in its place; or whether
the effort is not on both sides part of that blind
struggle towards political security which for generations has marked the international anarchy,
and which that anarchy ultimately compels.

(9) The insistent belief that the simple destruction of Hitlerism will of itself free us from
the evils for which it stands is an insidious and
dangerous fallacy. We have slipped into the habit
of speaking of "freeing Europe from the menace
of recurrent aggressions," as though that would
automatically be achieved by the defeat of Germany in war. Yet we know that such an assumption, far from being self-evident, as we seem to

assume, is completely disproved by the plainest experience. In 1914, also, we believed that the simple defeat of Germany and the destruction of Kaiserism would free the world. Kaiserism was destroyed. We did not get something better, but something worse; more evil, more menacing. Only the political wisdom of ordinary folk, can save us from a repetition of the tragedy.

(10) If the civilian fails in that wisdom he will have let the soldier down. All the soldier can do is to bring us victory (if we, the civilians, make it politically possible for him so to do). To misuse victory will have made the soldier's sacrifice vain; his torments or his death, once more of no avail.

§

To that summary of the book's main themes may be added a line or two.

To sit down and write a book which should be mainly a fierce indictment of the evil of the enemy and a statement of the valour and virtue of the conduct of one's own country would be heartening and cheering to writer and reader alike; and not without its value as a tonic in the dull or agonizing days of war. This author has not even tried to write that kind of book; for others can do it so much better. But he has tried to show how certain truths, certain principles of conduct which he has studied and discussed ever since the years immediately preceding the last war, apply to our present situation; can be applied to the development of a policy which may shorten this war, render our side victorious in it, and ensure that it shall not have to be fought all over again.

That is task enough.

CHAPTER II

THE PRIMARY CONDITION OF SUCCESS

The job of the civilian in this war is to see that the victory which the soldier brings is not thrown away and rendered useless, as the last victory was, by political stupidity rooted in easily aroused emotions of hate and retaliation swamping common sense. The warnings of the danger of mere animal pugnacity uttered during the last war, were disregarded—are the same warnings to be disregarded again?

1918-1939

EARLY in May, 1918, some six months before the termination of the last war, there appeared a book by the present writer entitled *The Political Conditions of Allied Success: A Plea for the Protective Union of the Democracies.*[1]

The author there pointed out that if the work of the soldiers was to be fruitful, was to accomplish ends commensurate with the greatness of their sacrifice, certain political conditions had to

[1] Putnam & Sons, London and New York. It is a very absurd convention which condemns as bad taste the mention by an author of his own previous work. If a writer is engaged during thirty years elucidating certain political principles, and events during that period throw light upon them, the fact is an important part of the material needed by the reader for the formation of a judgment.

be fulfilled; that it was for us, the civilians, to fulfil those conditions, since the soldiers could not; that so to do was indeed a solemn duty we owed them. The author went on to indicate what he thought the conditions of success were (they are particularized at points in this present book), to predict that failure to fulfil them would render our victory of little permanent avail, and would compel us one day to fight the war all over again. Those conditions were not fulfilled, and we are now being compelled to fight the war all over again.

In the preface of the twenty-year-old book the author indicates why he feared the public would not give adequate attention in time to the political side of the task they had undertaken. "The most serious obstacle which the argument of this book has to encounter," he wrote, "is a temperamental one—the emotional condition of most of us in war time."

That mood is apt to lead us into one of two misunderstandings in considering recommendations such as those here urged: either to the decision that they are presented as an alternative to the active prosecution of the war, and are thus, in however elusive or disguised a form, counsels of surrender; or, if we escape that misunderstanding and realize that the arguments favour the active waging of the war, to the decision that they are superfluous for those already convinced of the need of victory.

In attempting to forestall both of these misinterpretations, he went on, I have risked the reader's weariness and irritation by an insistent iteration of these things. The policies here discussed are not put forward as an alternative to the active prosecution of the war, but as the indispensable condition of its success; not as a substitute for the military power of the Alliance, but as the means by which that power can be made effective, now and in the future. (pp. iii-iv.)

Categoric as that was, he did not have much hope, he went on to explain, that it would suffice to prevent the misinterpretations already indicated. "For the temperamental obstacle goes deeper than an intellectual misinterpretation. It is rooted perhaps in an elemental desire to give emotions free play, and to escape the discipline and responsibilities—and uncertainties—of intellectual decisions." And he put this question: "Can an alliance of democracies wage war successfully if its public opinion yields to this desire for emotional indulgence and discards the spirit of political rationalism? Can patriotic feeling be a substitute for reasoned discussion?"

In the early stages of a war, the moral issues of which are as clear as they are in this, it generally seems to most of us self-evident that the only pub-

lic opinion which matters is the public determination to go through to victory. To be convinced of
the justice of our cause, to feel so intensely about it
that there shall be no danger of any failure of national unity, these are assumed to be the moral
essentials of success. You are for your country, or
you are against it. As to war aims, the easiest definition is M. Clemenceau's: Victory. "Realizing the
issues of the war" means understanding fully the
perfidy of the enemy and the righteousness of our
own cause. Patriotic propaganda is conceived in
those terms. Intellectual qualifications of any kind,
or any attitude of enquiry, are taken as clear indi-
cation of defective patriotism. It is felt that the
surest foundations of national solidarity and the
safest guide to policy are to be found, not in discussion and argument, but in intense feeling; not
in complex ideas but in simple emotions. As the
movie advertisement of the war play says: "You
can't put up a good fight until your blood boils.
This film will make it boil." We feel that boiling
blood is the best moral assurance of success. Such
is the state of mind of most nations on first entering
war.

But the experience of the last year or two has
shown us that in wars fought by democracies, and
particularly by democracies forming an alliance,
new situations involving new decisions are repeatedly presenting themselves; and for making those
decisions emotion is no guide. Emotion will carry
you along the road when the road is chosen, but it

will not necessarily help you to determine which is the right road. It may indeed be a most serious impediment to a sound decision. And even in the simpler kind of fight there is a degree of heat which may be disastrous. It is a recognized method in prize-fighting to make your opponent lose his temper. The resulting hot-headedness may offset superior strength or ability. The toreador manages to reduce an opponent twenty times his own strength by making that opponent literally "see red." And we have found that a war waged by a democracy, or, still more by an alliance made up of a group of different democracies, is by no means as simple as a prize-fight. The "boiling blood" of an emotional public opinion may be at certain junctures a very disastrous handicap. (pp. vi-ix.)

I have permitted myself this somewhat lengthy quotation from a twenty-year-old book because I find myself already struggling in the same current in which I found myself struggling in the last war, urging precisely the same arguments. In illustrating the relation of the political to the military problem I used terms certainly worth recalling in our present situation. These words:

The position of Russia alone might decide the future in Germany's favour. We are faced by this overwhelming fact: that while, during three years we have been impatiently disparaging "political strategy," the enemy has been using it to such good purpose that he has been able, by virtue of it, completely to offset the inferiority of the sum total of his resources; and if we could imagine his winning it would be a political success, based mainly on the alienation of Russia from our Alliance.

The whole Russian problem demonstrates that aims and methods cannot be separated; that opinions concerning them may work almost unconsciously in the public mind and effect the direction of policy and the unity of our alliance. Even definite military success might be undone at the peace table if we should there disagree as to our future aims: for the enemy would know that his temporary defeat could later be "corrected" as against a Europe hopelessly divided against itself (pp. xi, xii).

These words were written twenty-two years ago. But if they had been written twenty-two days ago, or this morning, they could not have been more apposite to our present situation. Which means this: That an issue, perfectly visible more than twenty years ago, has been evaded, and the situation created by it persistently mismanaged during all the intervening period.

Are we likely to be really victorious, or is victory likely to serve much if that evasion and that mismanagement mark this war as they marked the last?

When the 1914 war started I tried to secure some public interest in the kind of peace by which the purposes of victory were to be carried into effect, insisting particularly that the peace should not be a dictated one, that the German people should have some part in its discussion and be brought to feel that it was workable and just; and insisting also that the unity of the non-German world, the democracies, be maintained after the war. To that end, during the war, I made certain proposals, referred to later in these pages. (Already, before the war I had tried to warn the public that vast indemnities could not be obtained, and that the attempt to obtain them would have disastrous financial and economic results.) But all such efforts were deeply resented. "It is insulting to this country," remarked in effect the then editor of one very old and successful weekly review, "to assume that Britain will not make an entirely just and honourable peace." One great pro-consul declared that any discussion of the cause of war, or its cure, was futile. "There is," he said, "only one cause of war, Germans, and the cure is to beat them to their knees." Discussion of what was to follow the war was premature and useless. The arguments as to the dangers of enormous reparations claims were dismissed as "a desire to let the Germans off the penalty of their

crime"; pleas in respect of the peace terms as
"Hun Coddling." (The Press then was full of that
sort of catch-word, and this author had to face
generally bitter charges that he was a pro-
German, a defeatist, if indeed he had not in some
way been nobbled or corrupted by the Kaiser.)
Did he, or did he not, want Germany's defeat?

That the mere defeat of Germany would suffice
to bring peace was insisted upon. A characteristic
expression of the opinion of the time is one which
occurs in J. L. Headlam's book, *The Issue,* and is
as follows:

> Men talk of the terms of peace. They matter lit-
> tle. With a Germany victorious no terms could
> secure the future of Europe, with a Germany de-
> feated no artificial securities will be wanted, for
> there will be a stronger security in the conscious-
> ness of defeat.

That view, too, we can judge in the light of the
event. There was perhaps some excuse for that
error then. We have none now for believing anything of the sort. For we know to a dead certainty,
on the strength of tragic experience, that the mere
defeat of Germany does not of itself accomplish
the aim we set out to accomplish.

If this book embodied some technical criticism
of the management of the war—the faulty em-
placement of factories, or methods of air-raid pre-

cautions, or food production, or rationing, or war taxation—no one would object. Everyone would agree that the consideration and discussion of those things by civilians was in every way desirable, if only because intelligent comprehension of the reasons for a course by which civilians were affected, and in which they had to play their part was a condition of success. Even severe criticism of the military authorities by civilians (i.e. newspaper proprietors and journalists), concerning alleged shortage of this, that or the other war material, would be regarded as a useful service. But criticism of the management of the country's political position, consideration of the factors which will determine who is to be for us, and who against, examination of the reasons which have led us in the past into diplomatic decisions which everyone now admits to have been disastrous errors, are usually met with irritation and resentment.

What was it that precipitated this war? A sudden lessening of our own military strength? But in the months preceding the war we were getting stronger all the time. What precipitated it was a political change, a change in the alliance grouping of Europe.

Faults of policy may, as we have learned, cause whole armies and navies to shift over from our side to that of the enemy. Yet for a thousand that would be disturbed by inadequate arms not one is disturbed by inadequate policy.

Unless we become aware of the nature of past mistakes, have some notion of why we keep on falling into them, we shall continue to fall into them. If we refuse to look at experience we shall fail to be guided by experience. Yet as soon as one begins to deal with past error in order to try to see why we fell into it there is a disposition to say, "It's no good crying over spilt milk; all that belongs to the past." It does not belong merely to the past; it belongs also to the future.

The errors that we have made this last quarter of a century are not due to lack of knowledge or learning, ignorance of some obscure ethnographic problem of the Balkans or the Danubian Basin. They are due to the failure to apply to public policy knowledge which is of universal possession, usually self-evident in the facts of daily life and experience, but which we have refused to apply, because so to do would deprive us of some emotional satisfaction, the satisfaction of retaliation or imposing our will upon those who have presumed to oppose us.

The difficulties of this book are precisely those of the older one, then indicated in its preface thus:

Because it deals with the more neglected aspect of the problem and leaves the purely military side to those best fitted to handle it, it runs the risk of appearing to suggest that international machinery is an alternative to military power. In the same way, because it does not, in dealing with the moral factors, denounce German wickedness, it runs the risk of appearing to minimize it. But that denunciation has been omitted, first, because there is not much danger that we shall be allowed to overlook German crimes, and because the denunciation has been rather plentifully done by others; and, secondly, because it is the strength of Prussianism, not its weakness, which is the real menace for us. And its strength consists, not in its evil cruelties, oppressions, and lusts, but in the loyalties which, notwithstanding, it somehow manages to attach to itself. If it were nothing but crime and cruelty, it would not greatly menace us, for it would perish of its own weakness. Its real danger is that men die gladly for it, and as a mere matter of political effectiveness we shall try and understand how that is possible. To refuse to do that—to refuse to approach the thing other than in a mood of blind emotionalism—does not diminish the evil, it makes it more dangerous, for it leads us sometimes to spend our strength upon what is good and indestructible in our enemy, instead of upon that which is evil and destructible. Certain it is that these confusions are at the bottom of very bad mistakes which we have made in political strategy, and one is sorely tempted sometimes to ask whether they come really from an overpowering sense of responsibility to our cause, or from the sheer desire to satisfy strong emotional appetites at any cost whatsoever.

The times are too serious for looking upon our politics either as entertainment, or as the means whereby we may feed our emotions. The situation is serious enough to demand some moral and intellectual self-discipline.

Whether half the youth of the western world shall have died in vain, or to some purpose, will depend upon the understanding which those who remain can manage to bring to bear upon our international problems. That perhaps indicates the main obligation of the civilian to the soldier. It is an obligation which the present author attempts to discharge. (pp. xxii-xxiv).

CHAPTER III

THE SAME FAILURE AGAIN?

Even before the last war had closed the renewed attack of Germany was foreseen by some, unless certain conditions were fulfilled by the victorious allies. Those conditions were not fulfilled. They are to-day just as indispensable if the next victory is not to be as great a failure as the last. We are in a position now to see more clearly why the indicated conditions were necessary. And so perhaps fulfil them.

THERE are a few things which, if we had to do now, we should not do as we did on the morrow of the last war—at least there is fair expectation that we should not.

If, for instance, we had to write the Treaty of Versailles to-day, even though we are in war, it would be a very different treaty from the one we did write. Why? The facts were just as available then as they are now, and there were some of us who tried to make our generation see the facts. It is not that the facts were not then available but that the mood and temper have altered. We were mainly concerned on the morrow of the last war to feed a hungry passion of retaliation: we just wanted to hit back.

We are not likely to make that precise mistake again, though just possibly we may do so, if all the expectations of dreadful and unprecedented horror come anywhere near to being fulfilled during the course of the war. But in that respect our war mood is very much better than on the last occasion.

But to certain patent facts which it is necessary to recognize if our purpose is to be fulfilled, we seem about as blind as ever, to judge by the policy pursued during the last twenty years. Those facts were sometimes pointed out, even before the end of the last war, as indicating conditions which must be fulfilled if the purpose of the war were to be achieved and victory to be permanent.

It is, however, easier now to judge of the truth and significance of the suggestions which follow because we can do now what we could not do then: judge them in the light of the event which was then only forecast, but upon which we can now look back. The wisdom which then demanded foresight now demands little more than hindsight. Perhaps now, looking at those propositions in the light of subsequent events, we may realize, more vividly and clearly than we did twenty years ago, the vital necessity of the conditions there outlined. They were completely disregarded. It may be easier to see why warnings then given failed to have effect; and seeing now the cause of the failure, to correct it. If it is easy to be wise after the event, it is also wise.

A WARNING FROM THE LAST WAR

Six months before the close of the last war, in the book referred to in the last chapter, occurs (pp. 4-14) the following:

> The survival of the Western Democracies, in so far as that is a matter of the effective use of their force, depends upon their capacity to use it as a unit, during the war and after. That unity we have not attained, even for the purposes of the war, because we have refused to recognize its necessary conditions—a kind and degree of democratic internationalism to which current political ideas and feelings are hostile; an internationalism which is not necessary to the enemy, but is to us.
>
> For the Grand Alliance of the Democracies is a heterogeneous collection of nations, not geographically contiguous, but scattered over the world; and not dominated by one preponderant state able to give unity of direction to the group. The enemy alliance, on the other hand, is composed of a group of states, geographically contiguous, dominated politically and militarily by the material power and geographical position of one member who is able by that fact to impose unity of purpose and direction on the whole. If we are to use our power successfully against him in such circumstances, during the war, at the settlement, and afterwards (which

may well be necessary), we must achieve a consolidation equally effective. But in our case that
consolidation, not being possible by the material
predominance of one member, must be achieved
by a moral factor, the voluntary co-operation of
equals—a democratic internationalism, necessarily
based on a unity of moral aim. Because this has
not been attained, even during the war, disintegration of our alliance has already set in—involving
military cost—and threatens to become still more
acute at the peace. The enemy group shows no
equivalent disintegration.

No military decision against the unified enemy
group can be permanent if at the peace table it
becomes evident that the Western Democracies are
to revert to the old lack of consolidation, instability
of alliance, covert competition for isolated power
and territory, and a national particularism which
makes common action and co-ordination of power
cumbrous, difficult, or impossible. If there is to be a
return to the old disunited Western Europe the
parties which among the enemy favour a policy of
aggression will realize that, however much their
purpose may temporarily be defeated, the greater
material unity of their alliance will enable it sooner
or later to overcome states which, though superior
in the sum of their power, have shown themselves
inferior in their capacity to combine it for a common purpose. And that inferiority might arise less
from the pressure of any active agent of disruption
than from passive hostility to abandoning the old

national organization of Europe, sheer lack of habit
and practice in international co-operation, political,
military or economic.

We have ignored in large part even the more
obvious aspects of this truth. It was evident that in
the case of a war fought by a large alliance, success
would depend, not merely upon the military force
of each constituent state, but also upon the capacity
to combine those forces for a common end; upon,
that is, the political solidarity of the group. If one
member had one object, and another a different
one, so that they did not create a "single front," or
so that disagreement set in and forces were turned
one against another, it was obvious that the enemy
group, with inferior forces but more united purpose, might well have the military advantage. In
other words, the policies and ultimate aims of the
members of an alliance have everything to do with
its unity and permanence, and these with its military success during the war, and effective use of
that success at the peace table. Yet the need for
that unity has been consistently minimized in our
political strategy.

The factors of disintegration in the Grand Alliance are of two kinds: conflicting territorial claims
by the component states (illustrated by the demands of Tsarist Russia, Italy, Serbia, and other
Slav groups, Roumania, Greece, and, more ob-
scurely of Japan), and conflict of economic interest and social aspiration within the nations
(illustrated by the struggles of the *bourgeois* and

socialist parties in Russia, less dramatically by the revolutionary unrest in Italy, and even in France and England). These latter factors are more dangerous with us than with the enemy, because our historical circumstances have rendered us less disciplined or less docile, less apt in mechanical and de-humanized obedience.

The general truth we are here dealing with is of far greater importance to us than to the enemy. He can in some measure ignore it. We cannot. His unity, in so far as it rests upon moral factors, can be based upon the old nationalist conceptions; our unity depends upon a revision of them, an enlargement into an internationalism.

The kind and degree of internationalism indispensable for the consolidation of the Western peoples if they are to use their force effectively—an internationalism which must take into account the newer social and economic forces of Western Society—is impossible on the basis of the older statecraft and its political motives. For these assume as inevitable a condition of the world in which each nation must look for its security to its own isolated strength (which must derive from population, territory, and strategic position), thus making national interests necessarily rival. The capacity of each nation to feed its population and assure its economic welfare is assumed to depend upon the extent of its territory. A whole philosophy of "biological necessity," "struggle for life among nations," "inherent pugnacity of mankind," "sur-

vival of the fit," is invoked on behalf of this old
and popular conception of international life and
politics. Such an outlook inevitably implies an
overt or latent rivalry which must bring even members of the same alliance sooner or later into
conflict.

The only possible unifying alternative to this disruptive policy is some "permanent association of
nations" by which the security of each shall be
made to rest upon the strength of the whole, held
together by the reciprocal obligation to defend one
another.

The greatest obstacles to such a system are disbelief in its feasibility and our subjection to the
traditions of national sovereignty and independence. Were it generally believed in, and desired, it
would be not only feasible but inevitable.

Return to the old relationships after the war will
sooner or later doom the democratic nations, however powerful each may be individually, to subjugation in detail by a group, inferior in power, but
superior in material unity—a unity which autocracy
achieves at the cost of freedom and human worth.

The term "democratic internationalism" as the
condition of Allied success is not a mere playing
with words. Any understanding between nations,
even for the purpose of a temporary alliance or war
co-operation, is, of course, "internationalism" of a
kind. But the term used here means more than
that; it means that as a condition of our success we
must abandon the international relationship which

has generally wrecked alliances formed for the purposes of war in the past, and substitute for that relationship a different one, in which certain of the prevailing conceptions of neutrality, national sovereignty, and independence must be modified.

The newer policy can only become operative as the result of an "act of faith"—the conviction, that is, on the part of statesmen and public that the risks involved in the new are less than those involved in the old. So long as nations do not believe in the possibility or reliability of a new system, they will fall back upon covert or overt competition for preponderant power, territory, and strategic position which of itself creates the disruptive rivalry, anarchy, and suspicion, that destroy reliance upon agreement. By our own act in such a case, we create the very conditions which we urge as justification for the act. The one thing which alone will enable us to break the vicious circle is the general conviction that though the proposed system may fail, the old certainly will. Upon the moral courage to act on that faith depends the survival of the Western Democracies.

§

Why did we fail of the unification there forecast as the unavoidable price of success?

Just now it is fashionable to explain it by saying that the machinery we set up was not of the right kind; that the League should have been much more of the nature of a Federal Union. But in the very book from which the pages here reproduced are taken, it is urged that our League should have as much as possible the nature of a Federal Union, and suggestions are there made to that end. But, recalling through the pages of the book, the spirit of the Allies at the time, it is quite evident that any proposal for a complete Federal Union then made would have collapsed in a gale of ridicule; that the League asked of independent nations the utmost that they were anywhere near being ready to grant in the way of surrender of sovereignty. Even the more modest contribution proved to be asking too much.

It may be that the nations will be readier to make the larger contribution to-day, can be persuaded so to do. But this is certain, that they will not do so without thorough educational preparation; without the surrender on their part of prepossessions and prejudices still extremely strong; without the development of a political judgment, a social wisdom of which at the moment there is little sign.

Introducing the suggestions I then made for the more "Federal" type of League, I find in the older book this prefatory note of warning:

This book has brought into the foreground the policies and constructive proposals which, in the view of the writer, the conditions call for.

This must not be taken as indicating any profound belief in the efficacy of political machinery as such. The main factors in the problem which faces us are moral—certain ideas, traditions, aspirations, emotions, a certain sense of values—"public opinion" in the largest meaning of the word. But political machinery in the form of consciously created institutions is itself a factor in the development of public opinion, as well as a form of its expression. An idea or feeling—a religious belief or emotion, or the aspirations of a nationality—capable, it may be, of many forms of development, may express itself, in the creation of an organized church or a national state, and then be transformed by those institutions which thus become perhaps the main factors in the subsequent shaping of the idea which created them. (pp. 3-4).

If Europe has failed it is not so much because the constitution of the League was defective, as that popular opinion was not ready to work any international constitution.

We may find two nations with virtually the same type of constitution. One under it has order, prosperity, freedom; the other disorder, violence, poverty. The cause of the differences cannot be in the difference of constitution. A bad constitution worked with a sound political sense on the part of the people living under it will give the desired results; a good constitution worked without that sense can produce appalling results.

Our first task is to discover the roots of the popular unwisdom which have produced in Europe the results we know; and which, alas! might have produced them as readily, even if Europe had had a better constitution—which it might have had.

We shall find that the real explanation of Europe's failure is the role played by commonly-accepted ideas in the political life of Europe—ideas related to such things as nationalism, national right and international obligation; the place of force in international society; the effective means for the defence of law. And, as we examine these things, we shall find that the same order of ideas which has produced Hitler has also rendered much of Europe unable to organize itself effectively to resist his power.

Let us look at that point a moment.

CHAPTER IV

THE FOUNDATION OF HITLER'S POWER

*The explanation of Hitler's power is primarily the po-
litical incapacity of his own people, the ease with which
he has been able to capture their minds for purposes they
do not trouble to analyse. But a contributory cause of his
power is the fact that those threatened by it have not the
political capacity to unite in resistance. It is the personal
responsibility of free citizens to know to what final end
they are being led, to make their choice of ends.*

WE TALK of Hitler's power being based on force,
terror, torture. But he did not win his power by
force. He won it by persuasion, by a moral hold
over the minds of millions of German folk. Let
us remember that the Nazi party began as a party
of thirteen members in a Bavarian beer hall, and
possessed no "force," no material power at all.

How did it become a party of as many millions,
come to poll thirteen millions, even before Hitler
had become Chancellor? Because thirteen persons
were able to impose themselves by "force" upon
sixty million? The idea is, on its face, absurd.
Those thirteen, or that one, could only conquer
by capturing the minds of the millions; by a
process of spiritual conversion. Hitler owes his
power to the fact that he was able to achieve that

spiritual conversion. And even if we take the view that he was the tool of vested interests, capitalist or other, the power that he won for them was achieved by getting at the minds of the millions. The pictures that we commonly draw of the Tyrant as an individual or a little coterie of a few dozen "holding down" millions by force is in truth false for the force by which the people are held down is in fact force supplied by themselves.

If you think that a man becomes dictator by the mere fact of proclaiming himself one, you can put it to very simple test. Go into the street and shout, "I am dictator of Great Britain. Obey me." What would happen? The ambulance would come along, and that would be the end of your political experiment. But if, when a mob is surging down the street, a mob full of enthusiasm or spiritual exaltation, or vindicative hate, you say with the famous Frenchman, "I must follow them, for I am their leader," and you can then go into the street and capture their minds by shouting their feelings and ideas more loudly, more strikingly than others, then you may become their dictator and they may obey you. But you will have done it by reaching their mind to an uncommon degree.

The root of it all is the mind of the common man, and the question we have to ask is how it comes that millions of people, very like ourselves, just as educated, having had for the most part schooling during more years than English folk usually have, have put Hitler in power? A French writer has pointed out that "Even though Hitler never obtained for his party alone an absolute majority in a free poll, he came to power by constitutional means, supported by a coalition of Chauvinist parties which all had been freely elected by the German people; he had obtained at the presidential election of 1932, more than 13,000,000 votes, and his party was by that time the strongest in the Reichstag. Hitler's doctrine of violence and oppression, his bestial racialism, his glorification of war (in *Mein Kampf* he wrote black on white that the war of 1914 had been wished by the whole German people) have been preached in public from the outset, in millions of books, tracts, speeches. Hitler rose to power on the promise of a war of conquest. The German people were fully informed of their leader's intentions and sacrificed their freedom with their own hands."

We rightly distinguish between the German people and the German government, because while you can get rid of a government or a regime, you cannot get rid of a people. We can admit that the German people are responsible for their government without either hating the people (we, too, have been responsible for bad governments), or concluding that it is practicable or desirable to "punish" them. They have become obsessed by an erroneous but sincerely held doctrine, calling, not for punishment, but conversion to a better doctrine. We can best achieve that conversion by persuading them that our doctrine of international co-operation on equal terms will give them a happier future than their present policy possibly can.

Their main fault has been to surrender their critical faculty.

Their intellectual servility to "leadership" is such that they can be led to bestial cruelty, back to some of the worst phases of the Dark Ages. The essence of their fault is that they have surrendered personal responsibility for the policy followed by their nation.

They are not different in the character of their blood or grey matter from ourselves. We must not make Hitler's racial mistake. Their muscular tissues, their glands and physical processes are exactly as ours; the material of their brains the same. But by this surrender of personal responsibility, this intellectual abasement, they have drifted from one error to another, errors from which all their learning, all their erudition, all their externally imposed discipline has failed to save them.

It is a common theme of certain moralizers that our present troubles are the outcome of the personal moral shortcomings of the mass of men. Perhaps. But what sort of "moral" shortcomings? If the implication is that the trouble comes from bad intention, deliberate wickedness, lack of the will to righteousness or peace, a selfish preference for war as against peace, then it is obvious nonsense. Men do not from motives of avarice take the risk of being blown to pieces in their homes, or burned alive, having to witness the disembowelling of their children by bombs. The will to peace exists. It is frustrated either by the fact that men have mistaken the policies which might ensure it, have followed courses which, while designed to give peace have, contrary to their intention, given war; or because they have allowed themselves to get into a position of helplessness, within the power of governments who can defy their will.

Men for the most part greatly desire to do right; their difficulty is to know what is right. Mere passion of conviction does not tell them. Torquemada was sure that he did the will of God. Dr. Buchman who wants us all to be guided by God, as he is guided by God, and join the Oxford Group, praises Hitler and his creed as righteousness itself.

Our trouble is failure of understanding—usually understanding of very simple social truths, truths related to the working of human society. War comes not from bad intention but from bad judgment of policy, political incapacity, defective understanding of moral issues, "ethical illiteracy."

§

Every great war presents every civilized adult, virtually the world over, with deep and painful questions of conscience, not usually very easy of solution. They are questions certainly not disposed of by deciding, as some decide, to have no part nor lot in war for any purpose whatsoever. Even if the decision that war can never be justified is a right decision, it does not in the least dispose of the question which of several courses of national policy available is the least likely to provoke war. Very often war results from a policy, the honest intention of which was peace. War comes, not as the result of bad intention, but of bad political judgment.

The citizen of a free state is compelled, if only as a unit in the public opinion which ultimately determines his country's action, which makes and unmakes governments, to decide as between two or more rival policies, often not at first glance related to questions of war at all (such matters as tariffs, imperial preference, immigration, colonial government, reparations, sanctions, neutrality legislation), but in which wrong decisions may sow the seeds of war. As a voter he may have to decide as between two candidates, both of whom are prepared to use arms, force, on behalf of his country's interests or rights, but one of whom has a view of the country's interests and rights much less likely to produce war than the other's view of those things. What is to be the Pacifist's attitude towards these two non-pacifist candidates, that is to say, towards their respective policies, both involving the use of force? That kind of situation is an exceedingly common one. Is he to argue that since neither is pacifist he will vote for neither? But such abstention of high-minded persons generally in such situations might very well mean the handing over of the management of the country's policy to its most dangerous elements. Such a decision, in other words, might provoke war, and the citizen who took it would have his share of responsibility for the result.

It is the kind of situation presented to American citizens in the discussion of the Neutrality Act, as these lines are being written. Should a neutral country supply food and material that can be used for war purposes to both sides, or to neither? Is the cause of permanent peace, of justice, best preserved by treating both sides alike, whatever their respective merits? Or is justice best served in making some distinction? If so, what distinction? There are similar questions in great number which are merely evaded, not answered at all, by such replies as: "I am opposed to all war." As little, of course, are questions of policy settled by saying "all you have to do is to beat Hitler."

A curious contrast in the types of activity related to war may be noted: For ten who can be persuaded to interest themselves in the prevention of war, in the understanding of policies which lead to it, or the achievement of its purpose, ten thousand can be interested in war itself. For some years before the outbreak of the present war a very considerable group of critics (they included certain eminent personages now in the government), tried to arouse the country to the dangers of the diplomatic course we were following. They tried to point out that the end of that course was war. Their arguments were not answered; they were simply disregarded. And from the point of view of a party dependent on votes, or a paper dependent on circulation, it was perfectly safe to disregard those arguments, for the great mass of the public were completely uninterested in them. The "great public" of the two million a day circulation—the charwoman, the stockbroker, the milkman, the chorus girl and office boy—showed the completest indifference to the whole subject. Those who compose electorates which make and unmake governments were not at all stirred; so that the very powerful arguments presented about the danger of the government's course, caused the party leaders not the least disquiet. Prevention of war by political means was an unexciting subject which, to put it briefly, the "great" public neither understood, nor desired to understand.

But from the moment that war was actually upon us, that same public was immediately active and deeply concerned. The charwoman, the stock-broker, the milkman, the chorus girl and office boy all had things to do: they saw their jobs menaced, they had to get gas-masks, to volunteer for A.R.P. work. . . . And the whole attitude of the government changed. It might not be worth while to consider inclusion of this, that or the other person in the Cabinet in order to prevent war, but from the moment war is declared their inclusion becomes a matter of course. And from the moment war is declared millions who would not interest themselves in its prevention are pre-pared to give everything to ensure victory. In that activity they will show self-sacrifice, heroism of the very highest order. Each will show himself ready to surrender job, money, means of liveli-hood, life itself, in order to play worthily his part. But when the war is over, and there is a choice between policies of settlement, one perhaps specious, dangerous, threatening to undo the work of the war, to make victory of no avail, but also emotionally satisfying for the moment, while the other, which gives promise of achieving at long last the very purpose of security and peace for which we entered the war, but which also demands making first thoughts subject to the second, a decision of reason, an effort to weigh rationally one fact as against another—when it comes to that, the men, or women who were so ready to give comfort, fortune, children, life, will not give thought. They are bored to extinction. Men hate thought more than they hate death. And in refusing thus to give that particular type of effort, to make that particular kind of sacrifice for their country, their kind, they will have plenty of encouragement, not merely from that section of the Press which lives so largely by pandering to the first thought, from columnists of the Sunday papers, but from very pretentious philosophers, from certain of the learned and the literate. We are told by these latter that since it is the nature of man to follow his instinct and emotion, and reject that self-discipline which might enable him to guide instinct with some foreknowledge of its consequences, we must take the world, and man, as we find it, and him.

Such counsel is very welcome to a large part of our nature, and it is to that fact—the fact that we like to be told it is right to "think with our blood," that is to say, our passions, prejudices, pugnacities, irritations—that Hitler owes his power. "You like to feel," he says in effect, "that you are superior to others, that you belong to a race above all others in the world. So I will tell you these things. And if I tell you a sufficient number of similar falsehoods I shall become your leader." It is characteristic, by the way, that this type of demagogue, whether writer or politician, usually treats the common man with utter contempt. The author of *Mein Kampf* does so. "The 'people,'" he says, "quite plainly, are made up of brainless fools." Yet those who adopt this attitude usually accuse those who would warn the common man of the traps into which he is likely to fall, of superciliousness and priggishness, setting up for being better than their fellows.

§

The present writer is often accused of "over-simplifying the issues." Yet he is constantly finding his main task to be to protest against gross over-simplification of quite fundamental issues. Perhaps the most fundamental and the most disastrous over-simplification is involved in the ever-lastingly repeated declaration—particularly by eminent statesmen—that what we want above all is "peace." That, plainly, is not true, or we should not now be at war. For we could have had peace —the absence of bombing and artillery duels and raids and mass killing—on Hitler's terms, the terms upon which Czecho-Slovakia had peace.

One of the commonest declarations made by

statesmen in Britain is that the "greatest interest of the British Empire is peace." They doubtless feel themselves sincere in making such a statement. But plainly they do not believe it, for they deliberately abandoned peace, which they say is our greatest interest, and brought about war as the only alternative to submission to further conquests by Hitler. Which means that what we want more vitally even than peace is defence, peaceful defence if possible; but if not, then war as the means of ultimate security, as preferable to an abject submission to another.

If we had faced this fundamental distinction, faced the fact that we put defence before peace, the whole history of the long retreat before aggression, its condonation, its compounding of felonies, revealed by our policy this last few years, would have been a very different one. For in effect the Government justified its whole course, from Manchuria to Munich, by the simple question: "Did we not keep you out of war; did we not preserve the peace?" Had the public been more conscious of what it really wanted the reply would have been that it did not want merely peace, that it did not even put peace first; that it wanted national security, defence, self-preservation, and would have insisted upon knowing whether those things had been betrayed or endangered. And it would have added that since in the last resort the nation would go to war to preserve its security, would go to war when danger to that became evident, the undermining of security involved in this succession of retreats before violence only brought war nearer, made it ultimately more certain.

Throughout all the recent discussions one notes this particular confusion. We have distinguished between the Axis powers and ourselves by describing ourselves as the "peace-loving" powers, powers who did not "believe in war," and the others as the "war-loving" who did "believe in war." The thing was, of course, nonsensical. We, too, believed in war if we felt ourselves endangered, war for defence; and they certainly did not believe in war or want war for itself. Germany plainly wants to avoid war. What she wants is expansion, conquest, domination, power to impose her will on us; so to have us in her power that she can get, without war, any result which seems to her desirable. We are determined not to be in her power. At the moment we are less "peaceful" than she is. The real difference between us is not that she "believes in war" and we do not. The difference is in what we each regard as "defence."

Are we clear as to what we mean by defence? Germany is not attacking us—any more than she was attacking us in 1914. She is not attacking France, and would be delighted to make peace with the latter immediately. It is true that we fight for what this writer (for one) regards as a principle indispensable to civilization. But a month before war began those who now uphold the principle were attacking it as dangerous and unpractical, and treating very abusively indeed those who then upheld it. There took place, we are told, a revolution in our foreign policy in March last. It is important to know whether it was also a real revolution in ideas and in moral value. For if not, it will not last, and will be as unstable as the various moral and ideological "revolutions" in Germany and Russia.

How deep is the moral confusion in the minds of the belligerent peoples is revealed by what is perhaps the most amazing of all the features of the amazing history of 1939, namely, the ease with which the ideologies of whole nations can be turned completely upside down from one day to another; the way in which the loathsome heresy of Monday can become a quite readily accepted orthodoxy on Tuesday. For years, ever since the foundation of the German National Socialist Party, Bolshevism has been proclaimed by the Nazis as a foul moral pestilence, incompatible with human decency, with which no German should ever have contact. The destruction of Bolshevism was proclaimed as a sacred duty of the German people. For Germany to come to terms with it, still more to come to any sort of

co-operation or alliance with it (this is one of the
repeated warnings of *Mein Kampf*) would mean
the destruction of the Fatherland. Yet, on a given
day, without warning, the Führer announced that
he had come to what amounts in fact to an alliance with this moral pestilence: Bolshevist Russia
and Nazi Germany have proclaimed deep friend-
ship. Nothing, it is declared, shall henceforth
separate them.

The years of indoctrination to the effect that
such a union would be against nature, morally
revolting, ending in the deserved destruction of
Germany, do not seem to have mattered in the
least. The docile seventy millions accepted the
new doctrine as readily as they had accepted the
old.

On the Bolshevist side, among the adherents of
Communism, we see a result not less startling.
Two main elements in the Communists' philosophy had always been given especial emphasis.
They were that virtually all war between nations
arose as the result of the clash of rival capitalisms,
the result of the struggle of the capitalist order
for markets and profits, and more recently, that
Fascism, whether of the Italian or German order
was the last effort of Capitalism to preserve its
power as against the rising power of the proletariat. It was the business of the workers of the
world to replace the war of nations by the class

war, and to unite in common against Fascism and
Nazism, and bring the struggle of capitalist imperialism for territorial expansion to an end.

We have seen a Communist State enter upon a
series of territorial annexations, conquests and
dominations which had they been undertaken
by a "capitalist" government would have been
roundly denounced by the Marxist as the most
brutal of imperialism. A Communist State has
entered into alliance for sharing the spoils of
conquest with the most powerful Fascist State of
the world. In a later chapter the motives which
have prompted this are analysed objectively, an
attempt made to understand them. If we accept
the morals of the international anarchy, Stalin's
conduct is both explainable and justifiable. But
it makes nonsense of much that orthodox Marxists
have been preaching with dogmatism and passion.
Yet a hundred and sixty million Marxists seem to
have been as little disturbed by the fact as seventy
million Nazis have been by the complete and utter
repudiation of the thesis of *Mein Kampf*. The
only inconvenience the two dictators have to face
is each a new "purge": in Germany, the places
vacated by Communists in the Concentration
Camps are promptly occupied by Nazis who show
a now inconvenient anti-Communist bias, after
the party has duly directed a new "orientation";
while in Russia, we are told, the Arctic prisons are

being filled by those inconveniently hostile to conquest in company with the leading Fascist power.

The spectacle that should disturb us is this: two great peoples, one of them always regarded as the most educated, scholastically most drilled, the most academic and learned of all the world, so conditioned morally and intellectually that they could acquiesce in the complete overturn from one day to another, of a faith held, up till then, with passion; so that, what was right on Monday becomes wrong on Tuesday, and wrong on Tuesday right on Wednesday. It is the measure of the moral chaos of our time.

These somersaults are inexplicable save on one ground: that there is no reasoned conviction underlying these ideologies at all on the part of the great masses. The doctrines have come to represent either sheer intellectual confusion, or a servile acquiescence in the intellectual and moral leadership of violent-minded men, a puppet-like reaction to emotional appeal, a willingness to "think with your blood"; which is not thought at all. Is that to characterize us too, either during this war or at its end?

CHAPTER V

SUPPOSE WE SUBMIT?

Hitler goes on offering peace, especially to France, and if the impression grows that another victory over Germany will not make the lesser states like Czecho-Slovakia and Poland much more secure than the last victory did, the temptation to accept these offers will correspondingly grow. But a peace of submission would mean for Britain and France what it did for Czecho-Slovakia. We should not accept it peacefully for long. Why the Pacifist solution would fail to keep even peace. The Nazi phenomenon compels reconsideration of certain Pacifist assumptions.

BY NO means all the proposals for conference with Germany, or a truce, or an armistice, are equivalent to suggestions for submission to Germany's power. Still less does the proposal to maintain the closest possible contact with Russia, as yet neutral, amount to submission. But undoubtedly some of the suggestions for a peace conference at this juncture would amount to "another Munich," another application of the doctrine that it is best to get peace when it is offered you (Hitler's offer of peace to France is now a daily offer, blared across No Man's Land with loudspeakers established in the Siegfried Line), since a war postponed may be a war prevented, and since the future, even the future which would follow our victory, is extremely uncertain.

Indeed, apart from those who stand bluntly for the pacifist solution, there are very many who, taking into account that uncertainty as to what is to follow our victory, and the tremendous burdens which a long war will involve, hesitate between the two alternatives presented: one, a bargain with Germany now, before the devastation of our cities, before the mass slaughter of our civilians; the other a victory which may last no longer than the previous one, and after a short interval may have to be fought all over again. If, as time goes on, those appear to be the alternatives, then it is quite certain that a greatly increasing number will choose the former.

And indeed, they would be right; assuming it to be true that the next victory is to be like the last, no more permanent, no more fruitful of peace and security. Then, indeed, it were better to accept Hitler's offer of peace now, accept its risks, and meet afterwards as best we may, the problems involved, than to take the risks of a prolonged and costly war which, among other possible results, may leave Russia master of Europe.

We must face, therefore, this question: What would peace now, on the basis of accepting Hitler's latest conquest as his other conquests have been accepted, involve?

Hitler would certainly agree *at this stage* to leave the French and British Empires intact (if he asked for the return of the former German colonies he would argue that they are not part of the British or French Empires). It is further argued that any real domination of Europe by Germany would be opposed by Russia, whose position would then be threatened, and, if any attempted domination of the world were attempted, would be opposed by the United States as well; and that not even the Reich could face a combination of Russia, the British and French Empires and the United States.

At no stage would Hitler ask for the domination of Europe or the world, or admit that he was seeking it; and indeed not one step in the series could be interpreted as such a challenge to Europe or the world. Hitler might well be perfectly sincere in denying any such intention. The annexation of Austria was not in his view an attempt to dominate Europe but to incorporate a German people within the Reich; so with Sudetenland; so with Danzig; so with the Polish Corridor. The occupation of Bohemia, Moravia, Poland were strategic measures designed to secure the safety of the Reich. But the reply to these measures by Russia was a corresponding increase in *her* territorial dominion; and that increase in its turn will have to be replied to by Germany. And, given the international anarchy, these retorts will be, alike on the part of Russia and of Germany, justifiable. But the end of the process means the swallowing or the subjugation of the free states of Europe. For them to wait before taking action until Germany (or, for that matter Russia) definitely, consciously or overtly challenges Europe, will be to wait until it is too late.[1]

Suppose now that we accepted Hitler's offer, recognized the rape of Poland, as we have recognized the rape of Manchuria, and Abyssinia and China, and Austria and Albania and Czecho-Slovakia, then the complete disintegration of non-German Europe would be certain; free Europe's capacity to combine to resist any demand that Hitler might make would be definitely at an end. His bloodless conquests would continue. Submission now would mean that we should not, perhaps could not resist any demand whatsoever.

Hitler has, in *Mein Kampf*,[2] a passage which reveals real insight and penetration. It is as follows:

> A clever conqueror will always, if possible, impose his demands on the conquered by instalments. For a people that makes a voluntary surrender saps its own character; and with such a people you can

[1] The point is further dealt with in the final chapter of this book.
[2] One hundred and eighty-first German edition, p. 759.

calculate, that none of these oppressions in detail will supply quite enough reason for it to resort once more to arms. The more such extortions are suffered without resistance, the more unjustifiable it comes to seem to people to make any ultimate stand against pressures which appear each to be new and isolated, though in fact there is perpetual recurrence of them.

Now that is particularly true where the demands are made, not upon the same nation but upon a group of nations that ought to stand together on the principle that an attack on one is an attack on all, but do not; who are always saying when one of their number is picked off, "Well, after all, what are (as the case may be) the Chinese or Czechs or Manchurians or Abyssinians or Albanians to us?"

If now we yield, the redistribution of the British and French Empires among the totalitarian powers—Germany, Russia, Italy, Japan—would certainly begin, the first demands being "moderate." It would not be a redistribution by war. There would be followed the technique with which we are now so familiar. Within France and Britain, Fascist tendencies would be encouraged. That technique is indicated in other contexts in pages which follow. It is the technique—employed both in Austria and Czecho-Slovakia—by which

Germany says to a party, or a political adventurer within the nation that it desires to dominate:

If you will form a party attacking your government, a party of revolution or revolt, trading on popular grievance and popular prejudice, we will help you. We will supply you with money and will help you to frighten your governments by threat of war. It will be a great chance for any enterprising personality, for young men who desire to make themselves the ruling party of their state. There are glittering prizes in such an enterprise, power, domination, rule, wealth.

Even if it does not succeed, the solidarity of the state is shaken, and while so shaken, some similar technique is pursued at the periphery. In Palestine, in the Arab world generally, in India itself there is plenty of discontent which a shrewd conqueror, proposing to break up the Empire, could employ and use. What has happened in Palestine and in lesser degree in India, in Tunis, Algeria and other French possessions, need not be emphasized.

That kind of technique has had, as we know, amazing, incredible success. If now the latest conquests were accepted, totalitarian states would know that the future success of this particular technique, of the distribution of the British and French Empires among themselves, would be quite certain.

§

Not only Hitler but almost every German thinker or writer who has ever treated of international politics and Germany's position in the world has come broadly to the conclusion of which a hint was given in the previous chapter, namely that, given Germany's special position, she has before her only two alternatives so long as Europe remains an unorganized, anarchic grouping of independent states: she must dominate the surrounding chaos or share it; she must dominate her neighbours as the only alternative to being dominated by them, as she has been so often, and so disastrously in the past, as she was at Versailles. As Britain has had to assert command of the world's seas (runs the argument); as America has had to assert command of the Western Hemisphere through the Monroe Doctrine and by other means, so Germany, as the condition *sine qua non* of survival, must assert domination of Europe. For Germany, confronted (as a German would put it) with semi-Asiatic hordes on the east, semi-barbaric "mongrel" nations to the south-east, is in many respects far more dangerously menaced than either Britain or America.

If Europe were an organized society in which Germany could pull her weight and exercise the influence due to her, Germany's role would be quite different. But no such society exists, experience with the League would seem to suggest that it is incapable of existing and so Germany has to face the alternatives which nature and history present to her: Dominate or perish.[3]

Now we must give full weight to that case if we are to understand, not so much Hitler's position as Germany's. We simply do not know the forces we confront unless we do. It is not the lies, corruption, bestiality and insincerity of the German policy and doctrine which should concern us most, but the truly moral sources of Germany's strength, the passionate convictions behind policy. And very passionate conviction upholds some such political doctrine as that just outlined.

The German case was once put to the present writer by a friend of Hitler's in these terms:

Suppose your country had suffered defeat from three main reasons: first, a combination of her neighbours against her; second, internal disruption; third, blockade because of inadequate self-sufficiency. I suggest that those factors alone explain our defeat.

Next, suppose that having been confronted by a tremendous combination of your neighbors *and* internal dissensions, *and* blockades, and having

[3] For the fuller development of this theme see the author's *Peace with the Dictators?* (Hamish Hamilton, Ltd.)

been most solemnly, definitely, explicitly, promised certain terms, you *did* lay down your arms, and then found that the whole thing was a trap, that you were not, in fact, to get those terms at all. You cannot begin of course to realize what that means unless you take fully into account things which I am sure most English people do not take into account, or have forgotten.

We had surrendered under certain promises— promises embodied not only in the fourteen points, but elaborated in speech after speech by President Wilson.

Furthermore, you three Powers, Britain, France and America had always prided yourselves upon being the democratic powers, anti-militarist, hating war, peace-loving, pacifist and liberal in your outlook. Particularly had President Wilson taken a very high line.

When we surrendered, many of our people genuinely trusted all these assurances. The three great democracies did not believe in aggressions, in conquest, in power politics. Many of our people were captured by these promises. For years President Wilson had talked at them in this sense. If they would only turn away from the old paths of militarism and power and force and warlike qualities, and become like Britain and America—peaceful, eschewing politics of force, seek security in things other than militarism—they would find peace and security.

So we laid down our arms. And we received the

conditions of Peace. I want, just now, to eschew all recrimination. But you know, of course, your historians have admitted, that those conditions were ruthless. Foch justified them on the ground that they were the sort of terms we had been imposing at Brest-Litovsk. But here we encounter our first disillusionment.

Some of our people (mistakenly, in my view) had shared the allied condemnation of German militarism and German military and political conduct generally. Your own statesmen had declared that sort of conduct to be positively Satanic. But now they were adopting it, actually justifying it on the ground that it *was* our conduct. But we had been told by you that it was all wrong, that that was not the way you acted. And then you proceeded to justify *us* by adopting *our* kind of policy. It was a notification to me at least that you did not really disbelieve in what we might call the Brest-Litovsk type of policy, only disliked *our* adopting it; did not really believe in self-determination, only wanted to impose it when it worked to our disadvantage.

If that is, as it must be, a common, a probably prevailing German view, the policy which results must embody three main principles, these:

(1) Germany must do her utmost to prevent collective action by her neighbours' combination; she could always face any one nation; only a

combination can defeat her. That combination she must forbid.

(2) Blockade must be rendered ineffective by a self-sufficiency secured either by conquest or the virtual domination of territory which can supply her needs.

(3) Since internal disruption and conflict in Germany itself means impotence (one of the factors which produced defeat in 1918), it must at all costs be prevented by a complete internal political orthodoxy. No political heresy can be permitted. One doctrine only.

Now, unless and until we can make a real European society those features of German policy, Hitler or no Hitler, will remain the constants of our problem.

In the first of the above objectives, the prevention or break-up of any collective system, Hitler has very largely succeeded. When he came to power the states of Europe were, on the whole, tending, under the ægis of the League, to unite in collective action against aggression: the Locarno treaties still stood. Hitler arrested the tendency of European states to unite by fierce attacks on the whole League system—in which attacks he had strong support from conservative and reactionary elements in France and Britain. He made it plain—in the Rhineland, in Spain, in Memel, in Austria, in Czecho-Slovakia—that he

could attack more quickly than a European combination could defend. He intimated quite plainly
that he could and would make membership in any
defensive combination of lesser states a very
dangerous thing. His pacts of non-aggression were
a means, under a pacifist guise, of making combination against him impossible. The signatories
in undertaking not to participate in war against
Germany surrendered their right to combine for
defence, the right that is, to give aid when another was attacked. The whole system of mutual
aid went by the board. These "non-aggression"
undertakings were equivalent to a promise to
remain neutral if Germany attacked a third party.
It was thus open to Hitler to destroy in detail a
number of weaker states, who could only defend
themselves at all by acting together. That right to
collective action they surrendered under what was
in fact a threat of war. The destruction of the
nascent collective system of Europe was Hitler's
first great success. He was well on the way to
fulfilling the first of the three conditions enumerated above.

What of the second: Immunity by self-sufficiency from the danger of blockade, *lebensraum*?

In *Mein Kampf*, it will be recalled that the area
in which the Germany of Nazi religion and myth-
ology was to find her *lebensraum*, her means of
life and expansion, was to the east, on the Baltic

seaboard, those areas where the Teutonic knights had carried the German sword six and seven hundred years ago. Except for the western half of Poland, all that has crumbled. So little does Hitler seem to think that that position can ever be recovered that he has actually withdrawn German populations that have been in those areas for all those centuries. The areas are now indeed occupied by the Red Army or the Red Navy, and, given the advantage which the defence has, could probably never be dislodged even by the German Army.

But what then of *lebensraum*, and where? Where is the line of least resistance?

However much Hitler may disparage international co-operation for others, he has found, as other conquerors have found, that he cannot do without it for himself, even if only in temporary and *ad hoc* forms. In the establishment of Germany's preponderance he is prepared to enter such combinations. The one reason, of course, why he came to a bargain with Russia was that he decided that he could not overcome her. Rochefoucauld laid it down that two parties who could never agree on anything else, could usually agree on the spoliation of a third. A beginning of such bargains with Russia has been made in Poland and the Baltic states. But since Poles increase at a much greater rate than Germans, it is not the land of the former which can afford the *lebens-raum* for the two hundred and fifty million Germans of which Hitler dreams.

How far can this principle of despoiling third parties be carried by Germany in co-operation with Russia? Russia's interest, of course, is not in the need for territory itself; it is in the need to ensure that Germany does not get too much of it so as to be able, on the basis of its resources, to establish a dangerous preponderance of power.

Russia might be averse to taking over sections of the British and French Empires (say India), and yet find it easier to protect her position in respect of Germany by doing so than by helping France and Britain to defend their possessions against Germany.

Of this we can be sure: If now Hitler can achieve another Munich and secure French and British acquiescence in the Polish conquest, then both Moscow and Berlin will become completely and unshakably convinced that the French and British Empires can be partitioned, as Poland was partitioned, if not without war then with only a resistance that can be overcome almost as easily as the resistance of Poland was overcome.

This view, whether true or false, is not necessarily based on any belief in the cowardice or even the military incompetence of either the British or the French. The Czechs were a brave, competent and obstinate people. But once manœuvred into a certain position resistance was out of the question. The Poles are among the bravest and fiercest fighters in the world and the Polish Army has in its history done amazing things. But once the Poles were manœuvred into a certain position, resistance was bootless.

If we are in the least to understand the minds of the German or the Russian rulers at this moment we must consider as perhaps the biggest feature in the whole problem the fact that Hitler has achieved the amazing conquests of the Reich this last five years bloodlessly or almost so.

The conquests which Hitler has made would in the past, in the days of Frederick, have involved for Germany great wars. Except for a three weeks' war in Poland they have involved for Hitler no war at all. Stalin's predecessors—Catherine or Peter—would have had to fight long wars for the territories which Stalin has gathered in without war at all, also in a few weeks. And if now there is submission, this technique which makes this bloodless conquest possible for the totalitarian states would have to its credit the most resounding success of all the great successes that it has had heretofore.

The whole achievement is due to the fact that Hitler saw fully what the Allies hardly seem to have seen at all. He knew quite well that the material power and resources of Western Europe were immensely greater than Germany's. But he also knew that that power could be overcome if kept divided, that Western Europe's immense potential preponderance was useless in resistance to him unless it could be combined; and he guessed rightly, that it would not be; that there was not the moral unity behind the material power to employ it. He believed—rightly—that to play upon its nationalisms, divisions, pugnacities and fallacies, would be a relatively easy task. He believes, he has every reason in past policy to believe, that he can continue the method of *divide et impera.* So long as he fights "one at a time," he believes he can conquer. (He is treating France at this writing almost as a neutral, and directing the whole war for the moment on Britain.)

§

In considering how far German and Russian interests coincide, we have to take into account a factor very commonly neglected.

Economic determinism, particularly the Marxian version of it, embraces a fundamental proposition which is broadly to the effect that conduct, ideas, policy, are determined by the way in which men gain their livelihood, by their class interests. Any strongly entrenched class or interest will, we are told, fight for itself against a contrary interest that challenges it. Capitalists, for instance, and the capitalist class, will defend themselves to the death against the proletariat, who must—so runs the Marxist creed—accept the challenge.

But there has arisen alike in Germany and in Russia a great economic interest, which is also a good deal more than economic; a powerful class likely to defend its position with as much ruthlessness as capitalism has displayed in the past; to reveal a class solidarity as great. This vested interest has even deeper psychological roots than those which gather around capitalism, or property; and is likely to prove more militant than any other vested interest whatever to-day, whether in Germany or Russia.

The particular industry, or business, or interest in question, which already supports an enormous class certain to defend its class interests ferociously, is the business or industry of government, of ruling. It embraces not merely the ever-growing bureaucracy, which is so great a feature of the life of Germany and Russia alike, but the professional army, the police, particularly the secret police, the Ogpu and the Gestapo, the innumerable spies, and all those who give orders as distinct from those who receive them.

Here is a vast industry which provides not merely income, means of livelihood (and sometimes very large pickings), but what men normally value even more: power; power in a direct and visible form; power indeed of life and death; power to wreak personal vengeances; to pay back scores; to satisfy that sadistic lust of cruelty for itself which the last few years have proved is commoner, more dangerous, more satanically sinister, goes deeper, than some of us had ever believed possible.

Property, private capitalism, may be a means of "exploiting the people." But clearly the industry of government—a very great industry, necessarily, in Socialist or Communist states—can be every bit as great a means of exploiting the people, every bit as much an "interest" to be protected against the encroachments of popular control, the attacks of an opposition, the undermining influence of criticism and free discussion. The capitalist may sack a man; the good Nazi or Communist sound with his party can not merely dismiss a subordinate but can slay him, or see that he is slain with complete impunity.

What we face in Germany is not one Hitler, but a million Hitlers, all having the right to command, the right to impose their will without question on others, the right within their particular domain not to have their authority questioned, the privilege of not having to answer arguments which may be levelled against their conduct of affairs, the privilege of putting in gaol those with whose arguments they do not happen to agree. Are they not likely to favour the foreign policy which gives most promise of the preservation of their system, class, and amazing powers?

If capitalism fought to extend markets, its business, Nazidom will certainly fight to extend *its* business—extend it, it would certainly hope with as little danger as the business has been extended into Bohemia and Slovakia and in Poland.

But Bohemia and Poland are minor spoils and the road to certain greater ones—in Russia, the Baltic and the Balkans—has been blocked.

The next Munich, if only it could be pulled off, would give infinitely greater prospects, nothing less than the French and British Empires, stretching over the vast spaces of Africa and Asia. Think of Africa, and the possibilities of extending that industry of government to its black millions. Think of the possibilities of India—three hundred and fifty millions needing "government," those possibilities, so neglected by the British, that the whole of this vast sub-continent, with those teeming millions, produces jobs for no more than just a few hundreds of British subjects. (In the whole of the civil service of India, running into hundreds of thousands of persons, less than three thousand are British. Not one per cent of those who run the government and bureaucracy of India are British. At least ninety-nine per cent are Indian. The whole of India does not provide as many jobs for Englishmen as do the chocolate works of Messrs. Rowntree and Cadbury.)

But think what the average Nazi, all the thousands of little Führers would see in the government of Africa or of India.

Now, if this were merely a question of the transfer of rule of Africans or Indians from one domination to another, I, for one, would not deem the resistance to it worth all that a great war might involve. It has happened before, and European civilization hardly received a shock. Empires have passed from French to British rule, Spanish to Dutch, Spanish to British, Dutch to British, without disaster to civilization as a whole. If all India had remained—as much of Africa has remained—a French or Portuguese or Dutch or Spanish possession, instead of becoming British, it would not, so far as the general fact of civilization and human freedom is concerned, have made much difference.

But that is not the issue here. The point which concerns us for the moment is that the interests of this new politico-economic class or order to which I have referred demand the destruction of democracy as an institution and a doctrine, its reduction to powerlessness. And, after another Munich, the democracies of Britain, France, the Scandinavian states, and Switzerland, could no

more be defended against Germany than Lithuania, or Esthonia, were able to defend themselves
against the Soviet power.

§

In trying to forecast how much freedom or
democracy might be left to subordinate or satellite
states by a dominant Nazidom—how much it
could afford to leave—we have to consider the
third of those conditions which Hitler has laid
down as indispensable to the continued predominance of Germany and the maintenance of her
conquests. That condition, it will be recalled, is
doctrinal unity in the German Reich as necessary
to prevent internal disruption. Why could not
Hitler, having secured the disarmament of the
Prague Government, have left it alone to govern
itself as a small democracy? Why had the Gestapo
to follow immediately upon the heels of the Army?
Why was the Prague government forced to deliver
up the wretched German fugitives from the Reich,
to round up the political opponents of Henlein?

Perhaps we could answer those questions the
more easily if we asked ourselves why a liberal
constitution like our own has had to apply not
very dissimilar methods in India and resort there
to what is in effect the concentration camp—and
the secret police. If that degree of repression is
necessary in countries subject to Britain, what

degree of repression is likely to be necessary in countries subject to Germany?

The form of autonomy which a predominant German power might leave to its satellites, would not, could not, be democratic. None of the totalitarian regimes maintain themselves easily and without resort at times to ferocious repression and to terror. The purges, the Ogpu, the Gestapo, are so many proofs that they regard opposition to the regime as a standing danger, only to be subdued by perpetual vigilance, by controlling the minds of their subjects. Just as the Catholic Church in the Inquisition days, with a far higher purpose, deemed it indispensable in order to preserve its authority to control doctrine at whatever cost in human agony, so, we may be sure, Nazis or Bolshevists (we face the possibility of a Brown Bolshevism under Hitler in Germany) will find the control of doctrine no less indispensable.

The existence of successful democracies, the standing proof that this regime of repression was not indeed necessary, that prosperity could co-exist also with freedom, all this would constitute a standing threat to the security of the totalitarian class or order to which I have referred.

The idea that the new political inquisition could allow the infiltration of heretical literature, the existence of great and successful heresy at its doors, with no attempt to suppress it, is disproved not merely by what happened in the Middle Ages, in the Inquisition, but by what happened in Prague and in Poland when the Gestapo became immediately the sequel of German conquest.

§

It has been fashionable in Socialist circles in our generation to disparage, to deride, the liberalism of the nineteenth century, or for that matter of the eighteenth; to treat Locke and Voltaire and the Enlightenment with a smiling (or sneering) contempt. If this attitude implies that the conquests of the Enlightenment, the conquest of the right to free discussion, the achievement of the political constitutions upon which it must rest, are now so secure, so definitely established, that we need attach no particular importance to their defence; that they can be taken as matters of course, about which we need not worry because no one can destroy them—if that is the root of the fashionable disparagement of nineteenth-century liberalism, well and good. It merely indicates an invulnerable optimism.

Is it a justified optimism? Circumspice!

If the implication of this disparagement of the principle of liberalism is that it is no longer necessary, that it has served its purpose with the human mind, has won such victories of intelligence and understanding that contradictory discussion, "parliamentarianism" in the proper sense of the term of talking things over, is no longer necessary; that the right decision can be achieved without it; that human wisdom has so definitely advanced that the process of free debate can now be dispensed with without fear of falling into dire error —if that is the assumption, then one would be interested to know on what ground in the events of the last ten years it is made.

The truth is that we have forgotten, if we have ever understood, the real case for intellectual and political liberalism. The case for liberalism is that man is infinitely fallible; that he arrives at the right decision painfully, only if he will submit himself to the unpleasant discipline of listening to those who do not agree with him; if he preserves the right so to do. And we are so made that if we will not accept that process, our decisions, even though we be very learned, like German professors, may be perfectly monstrous in their stupidity, their ferocious cruelty, their self-destruction.

To say that sincere men, really desiring to do right, can never be guilty of evil things even if they do not accept the discipline of intellectual freedom, is to disregard the plainest facts of human experience; to disregard the long and dreadful record of fanaticism; of what men can be capable when the doctrine they hold is also allied to personal and economic interest. It is to forget all the Holy wars of Mohammedanism, all the tortures of the Holy Inquisition.

We stand to-day in danger of returning to all those old dark infamies. It sounds dramatic and unreal to make such a statement. But the thing is here about us, around us, happening with a dizzy rapidity. We see ancient and peaceful and beautiful civilizations, like that of old Germany, the civilization of music and of fairy stories, of forest legends, of dreamy old professors, of songs on Christmas Eve, suddenly collapse and in its place dreadful pictures of the old professor and the great artist hounded into exile, or subjected to obscene torture; the Germany of gentle fairy stories becoming the Germany of the concentration camp, the Gestapo, of elderly Jews kicked to death in the streets by young hooligans, to the laughter and applause of those who gather round to witness the spectacle; the spectacle of the dying agonies of some old man or woman, whose fault is that of belonging to the race that gave us Jesus Christ, His mother, His twelve apostles, the Bible, the Ten Commandments, that gave to the west its religion, the basis of its moral law.

Those things have happened—are happening—now, in gaols and prisons and camps, that dot the greater part of Europe, stretching from the Mediterranean to the Arctic Sea.

They will happen to us, too, unless we resist,

resist alike the moral errors and the intellectual fallacies by which those things are produced; and possibly, it may be, unless we resist the arms which have become their instrument.

§

The first and last question which civilized men —allied, enemy, neutral—most need to have answered is, of course, this:

By what road may men travel to a secure peace compatible with the things they value even more than peace?

Upon the answer to that question depend not merely our lives, the actual physical survival of millions now living and millions still unborn, but the survival of any hope of happiness, decency, compassion, pity, mercy.

It must be a road which not merely will in fact lead to this end of acceptable peace but one which man can be persuaded to travel. There are many roads which quite certainly, quite obviously, would lead to peace, but which men simply will not take because they have got it into their heads, rightly or wrongly, that those roads are full of bogies, traps, horrors, worse than war itself. The business of persuading them to take a particular road may be so difficult and prolonged that by the time the persuasion were achieved, the world would be destroyed. We have, therefore, to face two quite separate and distinct questions in this matter: decide not merely whether a plan or course of action would, if adopted, give us peace; but whether men will adopt it. If our judgment on the latter point is defective, it is of no avail that our judgment on the former point is correct.

This does not mean that men's opinions about the feasibility of a given method are unchangeable. As the previous chapter tried to show, men's opinions, sometimes their most passionate convictions can be turned upside down from one day to another. Nevertheless we are left in this problem with the responsibility of deciding which of the convictions and values that bear on the question of peace can be altered; how readily and quickly they can be altered; which are, if not unchangeable, slow and difficult to change.

Particularly does that apply to the pacifist solution—refusing to fight about anything at all. The pacifist says—quite truly—that if his method were adopted by the nations, it would be the final and complete end of war. It is not only the truth but a truism. If men refused to go to war, there would be no war; if parliaments refused to vote naval and army estimates, there would be no armies and navies, no guns, no bombs, no bayonets. If there were no guns, people would not be shot and killed; if no bombs, no air-raids.

It is all quite simple. Too simple.

For, whether they realize it or not, men do not want merely peace, they want defence; defence against those who may not have accepted the creed of non-violence; or until they have accepted it; defence within the state against armed parties —of the Fascist or Communist order—who would seize any government that was unarmed and refused to defend itself. Such an armed party would make itself master of the nation, imprison all pacifists, direct the education of the children and teach them to love violence, to regard mercy as weakness and respect for the rights of the weak as an abdication of the rights of the strong and mighty. And if men feel that they should be defended against the violence of those within their nation even more do they feel that they should be defended from the violence of those outside their nation.

To this, of course, the pacifist, or a certain school of pacifists, have a reply: If the armed party within the state, or the invader from without, were not resisted, or met by mere civil disobedience, he would not do much harm—less harm than would accrue by resistance. And pacifists might cite in this connection (though curiously they do not seem to) such recent experiences as the French invasion of the Ruhr. That invasion, and its results, were a striking demonstration of the feasibility of the pacifist method. Invasion was not met by organized armed resistance since Germany was not then rearmed. The method succeeded in that the invader had to return without accomplishing his economic purpose and Germany suffered immeasurably less than she would have suffered if the invader had been resisted by arms. But it was the sequel in Germany that was the really enlightening feature of the episode.

Here was a case in which, broadly, the pacifist solution had completely succeeded. But that success did not turn Germany into a pacifist nation: it was precisely *after* this demonstration of the feasibility of the pacifist method that she became (once more it might be added perhaps) the most fervently anti-pacifist, aggressive and war-like nation in the world. The two events—defencelessness, followed by violent reaction against it—are related as cause and effect. In the years which followed Germany's success in getting rid of the invader without war, the one appeal to the public by political parties, which obtained the readiest and most overwhelming response was the right of armed defence, the right not to be at the mercy of others, subject to their will. In the midst of great economic depression, widespread and dire poverty, the appeal to provide for armies was a popular appeal, one that went deeper into the hearts of the German people than any appeal for the improvement of their material condition.

It demonstrates that the impulse to defence, the refusal to accept a situation in which another by his irresponsible fiat can determine your fate, is a universal impulse, rooted not only in a profound instinct of self-preservation, but in ingrained conception of dignity, of Right.

To base any long-term policy upon the suppression of that impulse to defence is to ask too much of too many for too long. And in truth not one single state in the world—not one—has failed to reject the pacifist solution. All, by the fact of their retention of their arms show that all are ready to fight even though the outcome be certain defeat, rather than yield without an attempt at resistance.

I happen to have put the case elsewhere thus:

Every nation in the world, without any exception whatever, claims the right to defend itself by arms. It makes that claim and renews it continually by arming. That is to say, there is no nation that has adopted, or seems to come near to adopting, the policy of non-resistance, defenceless, the renunciation of war for defence. The compulsorily disarmed Germany of 1920-30, was not less secure or less burdened than the present armed Germany. But burdens were assumed and risks taken in order to acquire arms.

This deep urge for "defence" is therefore something which, like the feeling for nationality, we must accept as a fact likely to remain constant for a very long time and take into account. It is useful to discuss just what it is we fear of each other, what we are supposed to be defending ourselves against and to point out the extent to which the fact of war defeats the purposes of defence (and which this writer began doing in the years before the War and has done continuously ever since). But meantime we must have a policy in respect of this universal, persistent, insistent, passionate demand for visible and material means of defence. It can be satisfied by two possible methods, one certain to lead to war, the other if generally adopted, reasonably certain to prevent it. The nations hesitate between the two roads and demand of their counsellors which to take. We must answer *that* question, not dodge it by saying that they should take neither road, that the demand for armed defence is one that ought not to be made at all. Even if that be true it does not answer the question actually put by our generation. If we oppose the better method because the best is not adopted, then we have our share of responsibility for the adoption of the worst, behind which are the forces of tradition, habit, incomprehension, confusion. To support the collective method on the ground that it is less dangerous than the older individual method, is not to approve of either, or approve of war; it is merely to counsel that of two dangerous courses the less dangerous should be taken.[4]

The foregoing indicates a truth that grows truer as violence, such as Nazi violence, takes on ever more appalling forms.

The experience of the last ten years compels us to revise many of the underlying assumptions of the pacifist case.

Indeed, the whole issue to-day is less simple than it was. Errors as to the true place and function of force touch not only the problem of international war but also the problem of defending constitutional government against parties within the state, notably Fascist, who believe in armed force and certainly would not scruple to use it, as is proved by the behaviour of Fascist parties on the Continent in recent years, to overthrow an unarmed government. The first thing that would happen to a nation which had elected a government pledged to non-resistance would be, not foreign invasion, but seizure, or attempted seizure, of the government by Fascists. What would be the government's attitude? Would it bring the army, the apparatus of killing, into play? If it did, the position would then be that it was prepared to kill in resistance to (say) British Fascism, but not in

[4] *Peace with the Dictators?* (Hamish Hamilton.) The remainder of the chapter is largely a paraphrase of a section of that book dealing with the Pacifist position.

resistance to foreign Fascism; fight to resist a British Fascist government, but not a foreign Fascist government.

If Fascism, the arming of parties within the state, were to be met by a policy of pacifism, the nation would then have to stand by and see Jews expelled or segregated or maltreated, men of liberal or socialist views imprisoned, bullied, bludgeoned, bumped off, and—most importantly of all as bearing upon the success of the pacifist endeavour—children dragged into camps and schools, there to be indoctrined with evil theories designed to make of them willing tools of a totalitarian state. The prime fact we should have to face would be that that process of education would usually, almost invariably, succeed. The totalitarian state would educate a generation prepared to imprison or execute its parents for the "fatherland," or the "cause"; believe it right so to do. Again, that thing has happened repeatedly this last few years before our eyes; is happening now. An unarmed government would be at the mercy of even a small body of patriots honestly convinced (and the honesty of fanatics is usually unquestionable) that force to "save the country," first by seizing the government and then by waging war against its enemies, was not only justifiable, but a bounden duty incumbent upon them. Having seized the schools, the churches, the Press, the radio, they would make their will the people's will. So non-resistance would not dispose of the problem of force within the state; nor of war with other states.

That situation indicates the principle which should determine the use of force both as between parties within the state and as between states. Force should be used to resist the use of force as the means of settling differences, whether between nations or parties, so as to allow discussion, reason, law, to function. Force should not be (and is not in Britain) used to fight Fascism. It would be as wrong to prevent Fascism establishing itself by discussion and free election as it would be to allow Fascism to install itself by force. The force should be resisted; not Fascism. To argue that we "cannot fight Fascism with its own weapons" is to miss the point. To yield to Fascist force, to allow force and not electoral discussion to determine the issue, is to allow force to be substituted for reason. To resist by force the overriding of the constitution by force is, despite easy derision of the paradox, to use force in order that force may not prevail and destroy reason. Similarly, to use the pooled power of nations for resistance to the state which, rejecting arbitration or peaceful settlement, wages war in order to enforce its own partial judgment, is to use force to make peaceful judgment possible.

A further assumption which has to be revised is that war, aggression, arises usually from fear and sense of wrong; from economic strangulation and inequality; that the bad conduct of nations in this respect is due to bad treatment received; that Nazidom was born at Versailles; that as we behave towards others so will they behave towards us; that for this order of reason non-resistance is the best defence.

Mr. Gerald Heard writes:

> Are young Germans really Huns? Would they destroy hundreds of thousands of women and children in London unless they were told "England has 'planes which are aimed to do the same to your women and children. If you hesitate, your loved ones perish!" If England had no bombing-'planes which could attack Berlin, would London be in any danger? . . .
>
> It is fear which would make a body of brave men commit this abomination.

Mr. Aldous Huxley, citing the early Christians, William Penn and Gandhi, says:

> If you treat other people well, other people will generally treat you well. It is possible to go further and to say that, if you have the opportunity of going on treating them well, they will at last *invariably* reciprocate your treatment. . . .
>
> There is historical evidence to show that the pacifist technique is unquestionably effective.

Was it really fear of Abyssinian armaments which caused Italy to launch her war, poison-gas and all, upon Abyssinia? Did the complete powerlessness of the Abyssinians protect them from all the abominations of modern war? Did "unilateral disarmament" work in their case? Did Japan really fear the power of China, disintegrated by internal dissensions? Did we enter what was perhaps the meanest war we have ever waged, that against the Boers, because their arms threatened us?

But more decisive light is thrown by certain other cases. It is perpetually repeated that Hitlerism was born of defeat at Versailles. (It compels one to ask where French, Spanish, Belgian and Italian Fascism was born.) The most characteristic element in Hitlerite Fascism is its anti-Semitism. Now the Jews have been in Germany, or parts of it, for two thousand years. They have never been an armed community. They have necessarily practised non-resistance. For centuries in Western Europe they have submitted, virtually without retaliation, to persecution, indignities, infamies of every description. That policy has not protected them, nor caused their persecutions to cease. (Incidentally, the fate of the Jews in Germany compels one to ask, if Germans can so treat a German community, why should we expect them to treat any foreign community which happened to be as powerless as the Jews, any better?)

But there is an even more striking case which disproves the two sweeping assumptions about the effectiveness of non-resistance. There is a whole continent which has been powerless to resist European invasion: its people never having organized their force for their own protection: Africa. The negro has always been at the mercy of the white. No European nation has ever had cause to fear the power of a negro nation. What has been the fate of this unarmed and defenceless people? They have suffered even worse than the Jews. Transported as a slave to the western world, the negro's history tells the same story. Speaking broadly, there has never been a negro rising in the United States; the negro has never resisted by arms the fate meted out to him. And to-day, side by side with an Anglo-Saxon people, he lacks the most elementary human rights. What better behaviour on the negro's part is necessary in order to evoke that response of good behaviour on the white's part which Mr. Huxley assures us is invariable and unfailing?

But the negro's case is not the worst: the Untouchables of India fall even lower than the negro. The unbelievable oppression of a vast body of people, numbering more than the whole population of the British Islands, has been erected into a complicated religious system. They, like the negro, have accepted their fate without armed resistance. Has that non-resistance saved them from millennia of misery and oppression?

Mr. Huxley has cited the success of Penn's method in dealing with Indians. It would be more to the point to inquire how far that method adopted by coloured people in Africa and the Americas towards the whites has been successful; how far we have been amenable to it. The Europeans of the fifteenth century who went to South America were usually received with friendliness and hospitality. The Europeans thereupon proceeded to enslave and exterminate people who, like the Incas, had received the strangers with friendliness and trust.

It will simply not do to say that the conduct of the Europeans was caused by fear. Was it fear which prompted us to enslave the African? As little as it was fear which prompted the Duce to launch his war against the Ethiopians.

Parenthetically, the religious emotion did little to attenuate our age-long oppression of weak and defenceless people. One recalls not only the inquisition, the religious wars, the St. Bartholomew massacre, but the fact that the early Spanish invaders of America who wrought oppression and destruction were often intensely religious; as were often the British. Carved upon the masts of Hawkins's slave ship were religious texts, thus: On the foremast, "Love ye one another"; on the

mainmast, "Praise God daily"; and on the mizzen,
"Bear ye one another's burdens." We know how
his sincerely religious crews interpreted those in-
junctions in their slaving operations.

A word or two on the psychological case for the
use of force by the community to restrain the use
of private force for private ends may be added.

To refuse to the community—whether international or national—the right of force, to demand
that law shall be without sanction, is in fact to
pin our faith to the workability of anarchy. But,
broadly, anarchy which might work if each were
governed by supreme wisdom, asks too much of
too many. True, men desire to do right; but they
are confused, if the community gives no lead, as
to what right is; and their judgment in a dispute
with another is swayed by appetites, lusts, pugnacities, tempers. And if they desire to do right,
they usually passionately desire also to resent
wrong, particularly wrong done to themselves.
(It was not the lack of any instinct so to act which
explains the non-resistance of coloured populations to wrongs, but the fact that circumstances
made cohesion and common action for defence
out of the question for them.)

Men cannot be trusted to be their own defenders of their own rights. If force is to be used for
defence in this sense it is infinitely better that it
should be used by the community as the instru-

ment of thought-out institutions, law, and not
privately by each according to his will, his own
light at the moment of difference and quarrel. And
this is true, even if all punishment is fundamentally wrong. Capital punishment may be an
evil thing—I think it is—but it is better that the
state should perform that dreadful function than
that it should be the private instrument of parties
to the dispute. I would vote for a Bill to abolish
capital punishment unless the effect of voting it
would be to cause friends of the victims of murder
to apply the punishment. I have lived on a frontier
where a group of ranchers, suffering from cattle
theft and the activities of gunmen, have said in
effect to the authorities, the state: "Either you
capture and punish these men or we shall do it ourselves." The state did not capture and punish the
criminals (not from any pacifist scruple, but because the state itself was ill-organized). Lynchings, punishment by interested parties, individuals, were the direct result. Law, even when
employing frightfulness like killing, is better than
lynchings which employ the same means. It may
be true to say that killing can never be justified;
but even if that is so, the legal killing is better
than the private killing, the killing, that is, by the
lynching party, or the parties to feuds like those of
the Kentucky hills; better because it has an im-
partiality and coldness which the killing by inter-

ested parties has not; and because the problem of retaliation does not arise, or arises with less intensity. The Franco-German duel has gone on for generations. But if fifty-two nations really had restrained Italy in the name of a law to which she herself had subscribed, it would have been extremely difficult for the Italian nation to have kept alive any similar feud "psychosis" with fifty-two separate enemies.

Those who have suffered by lynchings in the United States have long pleaded the use of Federal power as a preventive. But the Federal Government has been "non-resistant" to the violence of lynchers; the negroes have had to be. This failure of the Federal Government, the law, to use force, has in no way deterred lynchers, in no way tended to discredit the habit. Had Federal force been resolutely used just once to protect negroes from lynching and frustrate the connivance of local authorities therein, the whole attitude to lynching would have changed; not so much because the whites would be "frightened" by superior force, but because the authority of law, the fact that it could be put into operation for the weak and the despised as well as the powerful, would have been enhanced. The fact that the American Federal Government was pacifist at that particular point and is so little pacifist when certain powerful white interests are involved, does not enhance the morality of the situation. The refusal to use force at that point makes the morality of the "pacifism" contemptible.

The nations of the League were pacifist in respect of the restraint of Italy: both Britain and France announced beforehand that military action was ruled out. Nothing, said Mr. Baldwin, would induce him to adopt a policy which might lead to war with Italy. Not one ship, said Sir John Simon, would be sacrificed for Abyssinia. This particular manifestation of pacifism in those particular circumstances did not lessen the future likelihood of further force, or the drift to violence. It increased it, increased cynicism; helped to destroy all belief in Right. After the recognition of the Italian conquest by Britain and the acquiescence in the Italian invasion of Spain a continental man of letters wrote: "We know exactly what it is worth to have the world admit the righteousness of your cause if that cause is attacked. The world's recognition of your righteousness will be worth precisely nothing at all." The fact that Italy "got away with it" strengthened every argument for the old international anarchy, all the cynicisms, the Machiavellianisms, the immoralisms which support it. Had the fifty-two nations used force to restrain Italy the precise contrary would have been true.

The reasons are plain. Force was withheld and Abyssinia sacrificed, not because men object to

using it, but because they are only at present ready
to use it for themselves, in shortsighted selfishness.
To say: "We will fight for our own direct defence,
but not for the defence of others or for the law,"
does not help to get rid of force; does not increase
pacifism. It only increases cynical acquiescence in
a shortsighted and self-stultifying selfishness. Had
force been used to restrain Italy, the Canal been
closed, mustard-gas stopped, it would have constituted proof that, after all, a European society, a
European unity, does exist, and that the old anarchy is coming to an end; that men are at last
coming to see that what it is right to do for themselves it is right to do for the community, for law,
for others. Not to do it does not diminish force;
it only places force at the service of evil, and
makes its ultimate abolition infinitely more difficult.

CHAPTER VI

WHAT IS THE BEST DEFENCE OF ALLIED PURPOSE?

Does it consist in telling the best of ourselves and the worst of the enemy? If this were a war fought merely for Britain by Britain that method might be defensible as a tonic for maintaining morale. But we believe that this is a war for more than Britain, and for that reason desire to associate as much of civilization as possible with us, and to that end we should show how the pursuit of our own security and interest—which is a country's first duty—and which we should frankly avow as our motive—has come to coincide with the broader interest of civilization. And if the world at large is to take our assurances seriously, we must show that we have the intelligence to see, and the courage to face, errors of the past, to the end that they shall not be repeated.

As THE writing of this book has proceeded, the writer has gained increasingly the impression that it is likely to receive the strong disapproval not only of whatever College of Propaganda Britain may possess, but of those who are moved by emotional patriotism. Already, apropos of previous writings, one critic observes that I "seem to forget that this war is being fought for England" (a statement made presumably for the benefit of the

French, the Poles, the Czechs and a series of potential allies whom it might be desirable to have on our side). Those latter critics are right in their disapproval. The College of Propaganda would be wrong—wrong if their purpose is to convince the world that our cause is theirs, worth supporting by them at cost and risk.

For such conviction will not be carried to their minds merely by showing that our cause is better than Germany's. That may be true but it is irrelevant to their problem of choosing the many different courses open to them: neutral neutrality, hostile neutrality, benevolent neutrality, alliance with us, alliance with the enemy. Those questions are not even answered by rhetoric about the nobility of our intentions and our purpose; by moral indignation concerning the infamies which can be so justly laid at Hitler's door.

Consider for a moment the position of a great neutral and, or, a number of smaller neutrals, seriously considering their position in respect of this struggle.

They hear a brilliant advocate compare the two cases of Britain and France on the one side and Germany on the other; describing in moving terms the depth and menace of the evil that we fight. Should not that satisfy them that their interest lies in helping us to rid the world of that evil?

No. For they will certainly recall that a great evil was "destroyed" in 1918, and a new system erected on its ruins: new states came into being and old states looked to find in that new system greater security than they had previously known. But their trust was grievously misplaced. China struggling with a new life for her could find no aid when she was menaced with the very evils of militarism and aggression that the last war was waged to end. France and Britain said they had no obligation to help China; no obligation to help Abyssinia; or Spain; or Czecho-Slovakia.

But Britain and France decided to help Poland; and truly their fight for her is a righteous fight. But how do we know, will certainly question those neutrals, that if we aid you in this fight, you will in the future aid us if we should need your help? Shall we just have to trust to your judgment—which decided that you could not help China, Abyssinia or Czecho-Slovakia? Do we risk the fate of those? Or shall we have something more definite, more dependable, more certain?

The case which we make must constitute an assurance on those points if it is to have value at all from the point of view of neutral support. And that assurance can only carry conviction to the degree that we show (a) that it is to our interest to establish as a permanent feature of European life that principle for which we now fight, and (b) that we are at long last, in contrast to our past behaviour, realizing that such is our interest.

The world as a whole—everywhere except in Germany and largely even in Germany itself—is perfectly familiar with the infamies of Hitler. But other rulers have been infamous: the world has not necessarily found it wise to make war upon them on behalf of abstract goodness. Nor is the question settled in the very least by presenting the proposition, now so common, that since the growth in power in the Nazi regime is a threat to free peoples everywhere all free peoples should unite in its destruction. Will it be destroyed by our victory over Germany? Some score of nations entered the war of 1914 or associated themselves with the cause of the Allies for the purpose of ending German militarism. The Allies were victorious. Their victory was not followed by the disappearance of German militarism; it was followed by its increase, its worsening. Nor is that all. Will the end of German domination be followed automatically by the beginning of Russian domination?

There are other contingencies commonly canvassed.

Are certain influential elements of the Right in Britain and France working for a restoration of the monarchies in Germany and Austria, and then for their participation in a new anti-Russian, anti-Comintern combination into which Italy and Japan would enter?

It sounds fantastic. But things just as fantastic have happened of late. Such a combination would, of course, meet bitter and probably violent resistance on the part of the Left, both in France and in Britain, to say nothing of the Left in the rest of Europe. It would be almost certainly the signal for a true civil war in Europe.

Discussions of such a contingency as this again raise questions as to the kind of international order for which British policy is to stand. Is that order to exclude states of Bolshevist tendency? And what is Bolshevist tendency? Would New Zealand qualify for that condemnation?

It is here suggested that if the international order is to direct its main effort towards establishing the right of every nation as a corporate body to be secure from violence and aggression, even though it be "Socialist," then it can succeed, and we can achieve order and stability. But if security is to be subject to the kind of test which certain circles alike in Britain and France would impose, tests which would exclude the U.S.S.R., not on grounds of its foreign policy, but on grounds of its internal policy, then indeed is Europe headed for chaos. It is here suggested that the concentration of effort should first of all be upon political security, irrespective of ideological differences, a political security which Russia sought for some years during her membership of the League, revealing thereby a readiness to co-operate with capitalist states. It is that co-operation for mutual defence without regard to the "class war" which we should seek. If we do so with sincerity, it will be possible to avoid alike the war of states and the war of class; but only on that condition.

We invite the German people to rebel against their government, to make a new revolution. But will that revolution become a Bolshevist revolution? We have seen the power of Soviet Russia suddenly expand, expand in a few weeks to a degree which no previous regime in Russia has been able to accomplish in whole generations. Will it happen that as the Allied pressure upon Germany in the West increases, her resistance to Russian pressure and Russian advance will be by that much reduced? Will Allied military success be in fact a success for Russia, a means for the spreading of Bolshevist influence?

It is plainly stupid to ignore these questions, to assume that the world is not asking them, and waiting for an answer. And no "defence of the

Allied cause" can amount to much that does not answer them.

Perorations will not do it.

§

Almost always when a war has broken out, there arises discussion as to *who* was guilty? In the case of the last war, great books were written and published to apportion the guilt between statesmen discussing, at enormous length, whether a given dispatch was sent before or after a particular interview; at what precise hour a government ordered mobilization. Such matters are, in fact, secondary. Our question should be not *who* is responsible, but *what*—what policy, what ideas, what political doctrine, what method.

Let us grant, if you will, that Hitler is the anti-Christ; or a glorified—and not very glorified at that—gangster; a super Al Capone. All that is true and well known.

Let us admit that in the years preceding the war, at Munich, Mr. Chamberlain was honestly and sincerely attempting to preserve peace. He failed. But to say that he failed because Hitler was a liar is a shallow and essentially untrue explanation; an explanation which is no explanation.

Every good patriot is prepared to lie for his country, not merely in war where, as the military manual explains, it becomes a duty, but in pursuit of ends in peace time likely to promote the power of a country for war, for defence, for survival. The patriot who will not lie to save his country is no patriot. The slogan, "My country right or wrong," was not invented in Germany. It was invented in America at the moment that America also was bent upon expansion. And it has been applauded and applied by every country in the world. There is no patriot prepared to say: "I would see my country perish, or be placed in great peril, or lose opportunities of increased strength or power, rather than tell a single lie."

For surely in that case he might be a great moralist; but he would be no patriot.

If one were a citizen of a neutral state (or for that matter of Germany) desiring to be intelligently informed, able to pass some sort of judgment on the policy to be pursued by one's government in respect of the struggle between Germany and the Allies, what sort of question would one ask in the light of the foregoing considerations? I suggest they would be some such questions as these:

Does the long term interest of France and Germany accord with a settlement which would broadly (particularly in the light of what happened in 1919) be to the interest of other nations, to the world as a whole? Have Allied Governments the discernment to see that long term interest if it is a fact? Will the electorate and Parliament upon which they depend permit them to carry out policies, ultimately wise, temporarily, it may be, unpopular? Will those governments be ready in the future to oppose aggression (and so aid states threatened by aggression) with the same energy which they showed in the case of Poland? Is it to their interest so to do?

Will their power on the economic side stand for wider economic opportunities for the world as a whole, or will the next allied victory be followed by still more severe economic restrictions, as the last victory was?

Any intelligent neutral (or enemy) desiring to get some sort of answer to those questions would before all else want to know what explains the oscillations of British policy of the last ten years; whether the "revolution" of March last represented a permanent change or a swing of the pendulum, whether future policy will once more be marked by bargains with aggressors at the cost of some weak state. If that imaginary neutral (or enemy) seeking for an answer in some English presentation of the Allied case were to find such matters dodged, slurred over, evaded, he would hardly be impressed by assurances that might follow.

No answer to the questions outlined above will

be accepted unless we are ready to answer, coming from the neutral world, this question:

Since the purpose you now propose was precisely the purpose of the last war, which you won, *how* do you propose to avoid this time the failure of last time?

It really will not do to reply that we must not try to answer because the attempt to find an answer would "create division in the country."

To achieve victory we must have in one form or another the aid of others, particularly of the United States. We shall get that aid only if we are able, in a relatively short space of time, to persuade, not President Roosevelt or his Cabinet (who need no persuading), but the great American public, without whose conviction the American Government cannot act, that our cause is also theirs, of America's peace and freedom, that of the world, as well as our own. If they do not get that conviction they are likely to hold back either until victory becomes impossible for us, or only possible at a cost which would make defeat almost preferable.

The case of America, although the most obvious in this connection, is not the only case in which aid, indispensable to our victory, will depend upon the degree to which we can carry to states now neutral the conviction that our victory is indispensable to their security. Never, perhaps, before has the outcome of a war depended so completely upon "who is for us and who against" —and who neutral. And that, of course, will depend in its turn mainly upon what others think we stand for, what our victory will mean; whether it will be like the last or something better; whether our victory having been achieved we shall afterwards tell them they must look to themselves for defence against the aggressor—as we have told so many states this last twenty years. The estimates which others make of our future policy—estimates based upon our past conduct—will determine their present decision as to aiding us, remaining neutral or joining our enemies.

Stated otherwise, the material force available for our cause will depend very largely upon what others think of that cause; whether they believe that we really do stand for a system offering better security than that which they could achieve by coming to a bargain with our enemy. And this leaves out of account altogether the factor of our own morale, the need for deep conviction on our own part that a war, more dreadful than any we have yet known—dreadful not alone in the extent and kind of tortures which it will impose on the whole population, but in the possibility of defeat —is worth while.

How can that conviction stand the strain of war; how, indeed, can it take any deep roots at all, if we have no grounds for believing that its outcome will be any better than the outcome of the last war?

Quite obviously we cannot stand that strain unless we have some sense of what victory can achieve, of how and why and in what manner it will differ in its results from the last victory, which has proved so tragically futile. If in the midst of war's appalling agonies we get the feeling that despite the rhetoric it will not make much difference in the long run whether we or the enemy is victorious, the feeling that both will be engulfed in a common ruin anyhow, that the next victory will, after all, be like the last—impermanent, unstable, having to be fought all over again by our children as the children of the men who fought the last war are now to fight it all over again—if that feeling gain possession of us, then we shall lose this war. We shall lose it equally if that feeling possesses those who are at present neutral; if the American public feel that our victory will no more make the world safe for democracy than it did before.

Herein lies the real war of nerves, the war of morale, of conviction, the contest of "which shall give way first."

Of course, we are convinced now that victory of itself will by some magic secure those things for which we fight. It is an illusion. Victory is a

means, not an end; a means which can be employed fruitlessly, disastrously, more easily than
it can be employed fruitfully and well.

We are beginning to say now what we said of
the Kaiser's Germany: "There can be no peace
with the present regime," which as a statement of
fact is true. But we may so easily confuse it with
a conclusion that sounds very like it, but is quite
untrue; the conclusion that to get peace it suffices
to destroy the Nazi regime. During the Great
War certain of our papers proclaimed the slogan:
"No peace with the Hohenzollerns." Well, the
Hohenzollerns disappeared but we did not in the
final result get a better regime than theirs, we got
a worse; and did not get peace.

§

On what grounds, then, are we to persuade
ourselves, our allies, potential allies, America, that
this time victory will mean something better, more
hopeful, more permanent than the last time? On
what do we base our hopes of that better outcome? How does our newly-created and rapidly-
growing propaganda department answer that
question? Will our next victory achieve more for
the world than the last one did?

We declare our purpose to be the freedom of
lesser states against aggression. We even ask certain such lesser neutrals to help us and to take

great risks. In doing so do we to Czechs, or Austrians, or Poles imply this: "We may win your independence by war, but there is no justification in experience for supposing that it will last any longer than it did before. We would remind you of what we have said these last ten years that we cannot be the world's policeman nor guide our policy by a foolish knight-errantry making the quarrel of every other state ours, turning every war into a world war. If you are threatened as Czecho-Slovakia was threatened in 1938, we can give you no assurance that we shall not "save civilization" at your cost as we did then—and as we did in the case of other independent states, even very ancient ones like Abyssinia?"

Are we really going to say that?

If the propaganda departments give no answer a great many semi-official protagonists of the British cause—journalists, eminent authors, editors, Cabinet Members, political leaders—give a perfectly clear answer. They answer by saying that the next victory will be just like the last so far as concerns anything that Britain proposes to do or can do; that it is not within Britain's power to do better with victory than has been done during the last twenty years, because during those years, run these pleas, she has done all that mortal man could to render the principles for which she now fights effective in international politics. With the present result. These advocates of Britain's cause propose to persuade America, the world, to give us their aid for another victory by insisting that we cannot improve upon the use we made of the last; that the next, therefore, is likely to be similarly impermanent. These advocates would have us insist that we have made the best possible use of our power since 1919 in the vindication of the principles we now proclaim; that we have made no mistakes in the employment of our power, particularly this last seven or eight years; and that such failure as there has been of world order is the fault of others, due to forces beyond our control.

If we maintain that attitude, as we are asked to do, it will in effect be equivalent to saying that the next victory will be just as ineffective as that of 1918; the peace no better; that we have no means of doing more than we have done in the way of setting up a world order.

It is astonishing how little those who insist upon the absolute blamelessness of Great Britain in the events of the last seven or eight years seem to grasp the implications of such a view. To argue that we have been absolutely right all along, as so many of Mr. Chamberlain's supporters insist on arguing, to say that the policy which led to the destruction of Czecho-Slovakia was completely sound and fully vindicated, that in Lord Elton's

words it "saved civilization"; to say that we should
do again what we did then, what we did in the
case of Manchuria, Abyssinia, the Rhineland,
Spain, Austria, China, Czecho-Slovakia, is in effect
to say: "Our next victory will have results just
like the last; help us to achieve it." To declare, as
does Mr. J. A. Spender, that there is no need for
any sense of guilt or failure in recalling those land-
marks along the line of our policy is in fact to say
that no effort of ours can render effective any
system for the protection of the weak against the
strong, can make it work any better than it worked
in those cases. And to say this is to warn those
now threatened by aggression that they seek co-
operation with us at their future peril, since it is
beyond our power to render effective and permanent any system of collective security in which
the small state can find defence against the great.
Yet the sum total of the power of the lesser states
—particularly in view of their strategic position—
is very great indeed and might make the difference between our victory and defeat.

It is argued that to call attention to these things
is to undermine national unity. There can be no
real national unity because no real comprehension
of our national purpose, unless we do call attention to those things and face the whole truth. The
ultimate indictment is not of Mr. Chamberlain, or
his Government, but of the nation, the electorate,

the public as a whole. If it be true that Mr. Chamberlain or his predecessors were leading us along a path the end of which was war, then it was the nation's business to get rid of him or them. It could have done so. Again and again it had the opportunity of expressing itself—as in the series of general elections last year; or for that matter in the election of 1935. Yet in last year's elections the outstanding note was the indifference of the public to voting at all. To judge by the sustained and increasing circulation of certain newspapers, the appetite for "soothing syrup" is inexhaustible; no absurdity of political view could nauseate it; not even when the daily expressed "Opinion" of the *Daily Express* was denied by the undeniable facts of the world about us; was a violation of plain truth, intellectual honesty, the simplest sincerity, reaching at times the point of outrageous buffoonery.

The faults which we have to face and correct if now we are to carry our war—whether "white" or "red"—to fruitful victory, are not faults of moral intention. They are faults of moral understanding. Some of our leading divines, moralists and moralizers bring against the public charges of selfishness, conscious "sin"; imply that if the will to righteousness were present, righteousness would follow in public policy. It is not true. Our people like most people, like German people, desire to do the right thing. The trouble is that they do not know what is the right thing. And neither the Government, nor its propaganda, nor the churches, nor, be it said, the Press as a whole, do much to make the understanding of the principle of righteousness in international affairs an easy thing for the tired, dumb and badly-educated millions to grasp; while those institutions do a very great deal to make the issue of righteousness confused, difficult, incomprehensible.

We are deeply stirred when Lord Halifax tells us, "we are prepared to assist those countries which feel their independence immediately threatened and are ready to defend their freedom. . . . In failing to uphold the liberties of others we run great risks of betraying the principle of liberty itself, and with it our own freedom and independence."

Admirable. But the principle of liberty was as much challenged in the case of Manchuria, Abyssinia, China, Spain, Czecho-Slovakia as in the case of Poland. But Britain, both by word and deed, rejected in every one of those cases the obligation to defend the victim of violence. It really will not do to say that we have in the case of Poland a power of protection which we did not possess in the case of Abyssinia or Manchuria. Plainly our power to defend, say, Abyssinia, was immensely greater than our power to defend

Poland. And if we had defended the principle itself where we could, we should not have been called upon to defend it where we could not.

The truth is (and if it is ever the time for facing truth that time is now) that the principle outlined by Lord Halifax has not been accepted by us as a valid and workable principle of policy at all until very recently. As late as March of this year it was repudiated with all the forensic genius that Sir John Simon could bring to the task. Once we accepted this principle of committing ourselves to the defence of this, that, and the other state, he insisted, we ceased to be masters of our destiny; the control of policy and the issues of peace and war were handed over to foreign governments. And we know that this plea was not an isolated one. As Foreign Secretary, he had urged, eight years previously, that the invasion of Manchuria was a "distant dispute with which we are not concerned" and as for Abyssinia, "not a ship would he risk" to defend her, that is to say, the law which we sustained would have defended her.

If now we avowed with some decent humility that we were mistaken in this line during those long years of retreat; that we ought to have taken the lesser risks to resist the earlier aggressions to the end that the later ones would not be attempted; that we now realize this, and that when Anthony Eden and others talk of the "revolution" of policy in March they mean just what they say, that our policy, outlook, attitude and principles have fundamentally changed—if we stressed that change, our moral position in the world would be immensely stronger. But this is not the line that certain eminent defenders of British policy are taking. They are insisting that what we did in the past was right; that we only changed because circumstances changed, and consequently imply that with a return to the earlier conditions of the world our policy would go back to its earlier method of attempting to secure peace for ourselves by bargains with the aggressor—bargains which involve that very betrayal of the principle of liberty to which Lord Halifax has referred.

Until we face the fact that we *have* been mistaken we run the danger of falling into exactly the same mistakes again. The very fact that for eight years our Government, a great part of our Press, a long list of eminent writers, lawyers, ambassadors, theologians have plausibly and elaborately condemned the principle which Lord Halifax says now animates the country's policy, increases the danger of reversion to the older policy. One recalls those arguments: undertakings to defend victims of aggression in various parts of the world make every local quarrel a world quarrel; it is a false principle to hope to "secure peace by threatening war," for then peace reposes upon coercion instead of conciliation, the coercion of the stronger party to the dispute. The very men who thus argued for so long are the very men whose task it now is to persuade the world that we stand to the death for the contrary principle of refusing to acquiesce in aggression and of defending its victim wherever we can.

Again we face faults not of moral intention but of moral understanding. To achieve that understanding is a condition of victory.

CHAPTER VII

FOR WHICH RIGHT DO WE FIGHT?

Do we fight in order to be judge of the rights we deem worth fighting for, and the right to refuse to fight for others? Or for a Right clearly defined which we will maintain on behalf of others if they will help us maintain it on our behalf? Do we fight to end aggression, or only to end the particular aggression that threatens us?

OUR desire is that our cause should be that of all free nations; and we point in justifiable pride to the fact that the war has arisen, not as the result of any direct attack upon ourselves, but out of an attack upon another state, on the other side of Europe, whose defence we have championed; and that consequently we do indeed fight for the principle of freedom itself, not less honourably because the maintenance of the principle happens to be indispensable to our own freedom, as well as that of others.

But in fact the free nations of the world, outside those of the British Commonwealth, have not joined us in that fight. The lesser democracies, like Switzerland, that managed by their valour to maintain their freedom, century after century, in an armed world; the magnificent little states of

Scandinavia; the Low countries; all ready to fight to the death for their freedom, and all knowing that the danger we face is also the danger which faces them, the shadow of which daily darkens their lives as it darkens ours, have not merely disassociated themselves from the present struggle, they had previously disassociated themselves before the war from any combination framed to deter the aggression which might precipitate it.

Why did they decline to remain in any defensive confederation? Why are even the lesser states that fought on our side a generation ago now holding a precarious, hazardous and threatened neutrality? Why have they dropped out from any system for the collective maintenance of the principle for which we now say we go to war? And why does the greatest democracy of the world still cling to neutrality—in the face of a criminality the menace of which is not the question for a moment?

There are doubtless many and complex causes which account for their line of action. But there is one which derives directly from our course of action, and which is consequently the one with which we should concern ourselves first and mainly.

In the light of French and British conduct, during the last twenty years, they are compelled to ask a question about the answer to which our past conduct (we may as well face it) has made them extremely doubtful.

The question is this:

For which of two ends do France and Britain fight: For the right merely of France and Britain to be free, or for the right of the world to be free because they have become convinced that without that larger freedom their own cannot be sustained? Are they determined to resist lawlessness and aggression as such, but only lawlessness and aggression when it threatens themselves? Do they fight, in other words, for freedom or for French and British freedom? If the latter, why should they ask us to help them?

If it be urged that in fighting to defeat the great enemy of freedom, they must be fighting for the world, then the reply is in the history of the years which have followed the defeat of Germany in 1918, and the position of the world to-day.

The mere defeat of Germany means nothing unless it is followed by some amelioration of the fundamental anarchy—absence of law and government—in international relations. When each fights, not for freedom as such, but only when his own freedom is endangered, then the enemy of to-day becomes the ally of to-morrow; the ally, the enemy; anarchy and violence without end.

The possibilities in all the combinations and permutations of the international anarchy are such

as always to provide a defeated aggressor with a
chance of come-back. What will it avail merely
to achieve "the defeat of Germany" (however
necessary it may be) when the possibilities of
to-morrow include a Russo-German alliance, a
Russo-German-Italian alliance; Russo-Japanese alliance (dominating four hundred million Chinese)
to say nothing of the possibility of internal up-
heavals?

Is it to be in the future an armed anarchy, as
in the past, or an armed society, an armed law
and constitution, however rudimentary? For this
latter we have in the past refused to take risks.

We fight for Poland's freedom, and on its behalf
accept dreadful risks, appalling burdens. But for
China's freedom from invasion and horror we
would take no risk. Our Foreign Minister explained that the quarrel was a distant one that
did not concern us. We flattered and courted the
invader; reminded ourselves that he had been for
long our ally, how could we fight him? Ridicu-
lous, absurd, monstrous. Besides, China's hands
(*we* decided) were not clean. Her state (*we* decided) was disorderly (our Foreign Minister
defended Japan so eloquently at Geneva as to win
the public compliments of the Japanese envoy),
so we put an embargo on the export of arms to
China, the country which had become the enemy
of our old ally. Abyssinia? Hm! Hm! Did not the

people eat raw meat? Why really should we interfere with Mussolini, so competent, so forceful, and
Italy too so old a friend? He and Bono were really
doing a work of civilization, explained Mr. Garvin, and Mr. Bernard Shaw, and scores of other
eminents. Let us put an embargo on arms to
Abyssinia! An embargo was duly put, what time
the petrol to enable Italy to carry the bombs
wherewith to disembowel, and the mustard gas
wherewith to flay alive the naked Abyssinian
peasants was carried through the Suez Canal,
which we controlled, duly paying the tolls to swell
the dividends of the shareholders, of which the
British Government was the chief. And at the
very earliest moment we recognised the conquest
and the Prime Minister and the Foreign Minister
visit the conqueror in his capital; banquets,
speeches, flowers, appeasement. So the conqueror, flattered, sends his troops into Spain to
destroy a legal government with which we were
at peace, whose ambassador had been duly received by our King, and who daily visited the
Foreign Office to learn that we could do nothing
to interfere with the invasion of Spain by great
Italian armies, or the destruction of Spanish cities,
and their civilian inhabitants, by German bom-
bardment (or, for that matter, the sinking of
British ships, and the drowning of British sailors),
because we had invented a new rule of inter-

national conduct known as non-intervention.
There was a committee. It met almost daily. And
non-intervention meant this: that while nothing
would be done to place even the smallest obstacle
to the presence of Italian and German forces in
Spain for the purpose of destroying the Spanish
Government we had recognized, we on our side
would sacrifice the right, long established in international law, to supply the legal and duly recognized government with the means of defending
itself. (We have supplied warships, arms, guns,
ammunition to half the governments of the
world.) So we were putting an embargo—a very
strict embargo—on arms to the Spanish Government facing the foreign invader, just as we had
placed an embargo on arms to the Chinese Government facing the foreign invader, the Abyssinian Government facing the foreign invader.

Yes, it was true that in none of these cases did
the embargo in the least embarrass the invader
and the conqueror, while it came near to completely crippling the defender; it was true that
again and again we had declared the sheet-anchor
of our policy to be common resistance to aggression anywhere; that we upheld the principle of
mutual aid in resistance to violence; and that in
such common defence of the victim of aggression,
of the weak against the strong lay the hope of the
world, of civilization. One day it would triumph.

Had we not said so many times? But for the present we stood by non-intervention; the appeasement of the aggressor, not aid to his victim; recognition of the fruits of lawlessness, not defence of the law.

§

All that is one-sided, does it not indicate the difficulties France and Britain faced? Certainly it is one-sided. It is the side which so many neutrals (including so many Americans) see, and consequently the side which we too must see if ever our advocacy or our propaganda is to reach their minds at all.

In each one of these cases enumerated above there was a great deal to be said for the line which the French and British Governments took, especially from the point of view of avoiding immediate conflict.

It may be perfectly true that the Chinese Government in 1932 and the Spanish Government in 1936, or the Czecho-Slovak Government in 1938, deserved all the harsh things that many conservatives in France and Britain said of them at the time. But the whole point is that we made the law subservient to our uncontrolled opinion of the merits of the particular case. We did not stand by a principle of law, the right of the weak to be defended against violence. We stood by our right to decide when the law should be applied and when it should not. Throughout, if France and Britain had been entirely honest, they would have said: "Whether we shall stand against aggression or not will depend upon whether we prefer the politics of the aggressor to the politics of his victim. We stand, of course, for the principle of the defence of the weak against the aggression of the strong. But we shall decide which weak against which strong. If we decide that China is not worthy of defence against Japan; nor Abyssinia against Italy; nor a Spanish government against a Fascist combination; that while we will not risk war for those nor for Czecho-Slovakia, but we will for Poland—all that is our affair. It is our decision, and ours only. We retain the right to intervene when it shall seem good to us, but we shall be subject to no general rule."

If that is our principle, then the world will decide that we do not stand for the principle of freedom at all; that we stand for something entirely different, namely, whatever in our good judgment, and in ours only, we decide is freedom; which cases are worth fighting for, which are not; for the supremacy of our decision in these things; not for any principle as such.

And neutrals will fear that perhaps just when their need of our help is greatest, we may have some new mood; may decide that their case is not like that of Poland, worth fighting for, but like that of China, or Abyssinia, or Spain, or Czecho-Slovakia, not worth fighting for. And that, therefore, the risks of accepting our promises of help in return for theirs to help us are greater than the risk of keeping out of association with us altogether.

And that, we now see, would be unfortunate. Yet, in fact, that is precisely the decision to which most neutrals have so far come, and so far stand by.

CHAPTER VIII

THE RIGHT FOR WHICH THE WORLD WOULD HAVE US FIGHT

The West has heretofore failed to organize itself as a society, in which the power of the community is pooled to defend each of its members against lawless violence. Civilization is increasingly menaced by the absence of effective defence of this right to freedom from violence and its threat; by the absence, that is, of a constitution commonly defended. If the British and French Empires clearly enunciated the defence of this Right, "droit," as the purpose of their struggle, they would sooner or later rally civilization to their side. But we are still confused as to that purpose and the means of its achievement.

THE question raised in the last chapter is whether we fight for the principle of freedom as such or just those cases of threatened freedom which appear in our good judgment worth defending; whether we reserve the right to pick and choose, to say that China's freedom or Czecho-Slovakia's freedom is not worth preserving at the cost of war but that Poland's is; the question whether we fight to have the right of such decisions or fight for the maintenance of a very different principle of a general right to freedom from violence. That question is not raised with the idea of indicting this or that government, for all governments have taken pretty much the same line, but for the purpose of clarifying a point upon which as the war progresses decisions of states now neutral, decisions vital to us, will ultimately rest.

Lord Halifax has announced that Britain is prepared to

> assist those countries which feel their independence threatened and are ready to defend their freedom. . . . That is why we gave our undertaking to Poland. . . . In failing to uphold the liberties of others we run great risks of betraying the principle of liberty itself, and with it our own freedom and independence.

(How one regrets that just that precise offer was not made by Britain on the morrow of the establishment of the League of Nations.) But any nation before responding to that implied invitation will quite certainly want an answer to this kind of question:

When on the last occasion you were victorious, you used your victory to create new nations or revive old ones: e.g., Czecho-Slovakia, Poland; you admitted into a system of collective defence certain other states, China, Abyssinia, Albania, Austria. But you left the potential enemies of those states in the greatest possible doubt, alike by your hesitation to give specific commitment, your general line of behaviour towards aggressors, the pronouncements of your statesmen, the commentary of your Press, as to whether you ever intended permanently to maintain your handiwork, whether the weak could really count upon your defence against the strong. Potential aggressors became convinced that aggression would not be resisted. And certain of the weak were therefore attacked and they have gone under. If we join you, how do you really intend to defend us in the future against the hostility of those whom you ask us to oppose? Is your resistance to aggression to be part of a clear, dependable and permanent policy? Do you give us categoric promises of aid on mutual and reciprocal terms, a definite, contractual obligation? Or must we wait and see, leaving the question of our defence to settlement at the moment of crisis and attack to your good judgment? Shall we in the years following this war, share the fate, if we join you, of Czecho-Slovakia and Poland in the years following the last war?

Now it will not be easy in any case to give the required assurance in a form which will secure acceptance; and it will be quite impossible if we persist in taking the line that our past conduct has been blameless; and that we could not have done other than we have done and that, it being impossible to do more than we can, our future policy will probably be precisely the same as the past.

In one of those flashes of penetration which make him so attractive and valuable a writer, Mr. Harold Nicolson has said something to the effect that the average Englishman undergoes actual physical suffering when he is asked to commit himself to a defined course of action in circumstances which have not yet actually arisen. The Englishman is furthermore proud of this reluctance, deeming that it indicates the possession of hard-headed caution; indicates that he has his feet firmly on the ground. "Wait and see. You can trust me to do the fair thing." That anyone could question his judgment as to what that is, is of course beyond credibility.

But there are other considerations in the Englishman's mind. "How do we know which side is right in a quarrel? The merits of the case are sometimes very difficult to discern," and so it must be left to *us*. We know these things, are able to discern them. And that is why we sent the elderly Lord Runciman to determine the rights and wrongs of the German-Czecho-Slovak quarrel; to examine how the German minorities had been treated, whether they had their fair share of government jobs; whether Czecho-Slovakia was any worthier of our defence than China or Abyssinia.

All that, of course, constitutes hopeless confusion.

When we fight for Poland, we do so, not because Poland's conduct has been good and that of her neighbours bad, but because Poland, like other nations, is entitled to life as a nation, entitled not to be destroyed.

Have we realized the meaning of that fact? Is that distinction really clear to us? If it is, we are fighting the world's cause, and sooner or later the world will recognize it, and in one way or another, in many different ways, aid our cause.

Neutrals would doubtless feel more certain of it if some of the spokesmen of our cause said bluntly and outright that Poland's behaviour has often been outrageous, and that that had nothing whatever to do with it; that what we are doing for Poland we are prepared, given the conditions which Poland has fulfilled, to do for Russia, or for that matter, for Germany. And neutrals would feel happier perhaps if a strange paradox did not mark our entrance into this war, the paradox that we have been pushed to fight for a principle which so many of us have declared a nation should never fight for.

Yet we have been pushed to fight for it, and it is that very fact which, more forcibly than anything else perhaps, will bring us to the conviction, deepened by suffering, that the principle for which we, like others, have so often refused to fight, is the one thing for which nations should fight; that it is the most vital, the most urgent, the most needed right of all; necessary not merely to culture, to civilization, to justice, but to life itself.

Let us be quite clear just what that ultimate right really is.

It is the right not to be killed; not to be flayed alive with mustard gas; not to be disembowelled; not to see the children, the very babies, gassed and disembowelled, because the babies' government happens to have quarrelled with another government; the right not to have to suffer those things, as the only alternative to complete submission to another's will, and that will usually the will of the most violent and the most cruel.

Surely that is a simple right, a simple proposition, capable of being made plain to the humblest citizen, the butcher, the baker, the candlestick-maker, their wives, and their flapper daughters, the charwoman and the chorus-girl. It is not a right merely to peace. It is a right to peace without complete submission and surrender.

Yet, if that one simple right could be established securely, the way to other rights would be cleared and made easier to travel. Until it is established, no other right can be secure. (It serves little purpose to give me all sorts of rights, as against my neighbour, if you leave him the power, which he knows he can exercise with complete impunity, and without risk, at any moment to come and bump me off.)

Yet around that simple purpose, around the defence of a right so elementary, have gathered complications, confusions, irrelevancies beyond belief. They are confusions, irrelevancies, due largely to erudition, to that curious fear of appearing simple which seems to curse so many academic minds, particularly—but not alone—in Germany. (To the present writer, once lecturing in a German University, a German student said: "Of the simplest thing in the whole world my professor could make something completely incomprehensible.")

The commonest confusion in this simple matter is surely not impenetrable. "If," says the objector, "all men have the right not to be killed, by what right do you propose to kill Germans? You deny them peace while they offer it to you."

It is just such simplicities we need to clarify.

We—British, French, Poles, Czechs—do not deny peace to Germany. We offer it to her on exactly the same terms that we claim it for ourselves: discussion of our differences, negotiation free from the threat of war, with third-party judgment if judgment is demanded; a form of judgment which ensures equality of right for both. Germany offers us peace on no such terms. She demands absolute submission to her will, *her* judgment; submission to her predominant force. We do not ask her to submit to our domination, but to the domination of the law; the same law to which we ourselves are prepared to submit. There can be peace from the moment Germany says she will submit her dispute with Czecho-Slovakia and Poland to third-party judgment.

Once more it is a very simple elementary social principle about which we are so direly confused. Its clarification is worth a parable or two.

In a quarrel with my neighbour about the title to a field, he comes to me one day, and says, "Sign this transfer of your field, or get killed—by accident, one dark night." If I submit, because the law is impotent and I have no protection, that kind of thing will be very common. For the most violent, most ruthless, least decent, will know that violence or its threat will be a short cut to getting what they want. My submission will not produce peace, for some, braver than I, will not be frightened. They will resist. They will get killed; their families will retaliate. It is all a very familiar story —of the Kentucky feuds, which go on from generation to generation, because of some quarrel over a fence, or a pig; of Corsica, with its vendettas; of Chicago with its gangs and racketeers. Submission will not bring peace.

But if I resist and say:

No killing please. I do not ask you to accept my verdict, so I won't accept yours. Let us put it to the judge, to third party judgment, umpire, impartial decision. The thing I claim—umpire judgment—is the thing I offer you. You need not accept it, and I shall not kill you if you don't. It is open to you, but you can leave things as they are, if that is what you like. But you shall not kill me if I can help it; and I shall not submit to the threat. For that would allow this matter to be settled by force, violence, or threat of force or violence.

And if the neighbours rally to my defence, making the way of the killer very difficult, but the way of the law open, he will in the end desist —either by leaving things as they are, or by accepting third-party judgment. But without that resistance the law would have perished and violence prevailed.

It may, of course, be wrong altogether for the neighbours to rally to my defence. It is arguable that they ought to allow the killer to work his will upon me. But what cannot be maintained is that the force used by the neighbours to defend the citizen's right to freedom from violence is in the same moral category as the force used by the killer himself in order to be his own judge of the merits of any dispute he may care to raise. Both methods of force may be evil, but words have no meaning if we argue that the purpose of force to sustain the law of equal right to freedom from violence, and to impartial judgment is in exactly the same moral category as force used to deny and destroy those things.

Is it impossible to make that distinction clear to the plain citizen?

Are the Ministries of Information, the colleges of propaganda, the British Councils, all the institutions of education and learning, all incapable of making clear to the world the nature of this policy, namely, that we stand for the right of men to be free from the alternative of being killed or submitting to inequity and iniquity?

For that is our case. We—Britain, France, Turkey—are the neighbours, who say to the killer:

Your title to the land may be better than your neighbour's.

But you shall not settle the matter in your favour by threats of death. You shall leave your neighbour alone, or submit your dispute with him to some judgment other than your own. We shall defend your proposed victim. For if your method triumphs in one case because there is no effective resistance, it will triumph in many, and none of us, not one of us, can be safe.

We do not care whether your neighbour is a nice man or not, a tyrant in the family circle, or not; keeps his wife on short allowance, or not; whether he goes to the right church, whether he goes to any church at all. These things have nothing to do with the question whether you, and you alone, in your sole judgment, shall be allowed to kill him, because he differs from your view of your own and so of his rights. You shall not be allowed to kill him for any purpose whatsoever, save one: to resist his attempt to kill you. And in that case we would protect you, as we now protect him. You touch him at your peril.

Is that an ignoble case? Or difficult to grasp, impossible for the plain man to understand? Would he fail to grasp the fact that it is just as good a case even though Turkey is not a democracy, even though we ourselves have been oppressors? Would he fail to understand us if we say:

We do not care whether Poland is a democracy or not. She was entitled to have her case heard, to have it discussed in circumstances other than that of being under the threat of instant extinction. We ought not to have cared whether Czecho-Slovakia had treated the Sudeten Germans well or ill; whether the Spanish Government was Communist or not; whether the Abyssinians really did eat raw meat, or kept domestic slaves; whether the Manchurian bandits were worse or better than those of Chicago.

We see now that all those contradictions were irrelevant. Men do not learn readily their real faith, and our faith is that the war-making must now end.

It is not a negative creed, just resistance to evil, as and when it arises, and only when, in our good judgment it has reached a point that demands resistance. The principle for which we fight is more positive. It is the defence, not of undefined right; for men differ much as to what abstract right is; but of one clearly defined and definite right—the right to defence from violence, war, death. For that right we stand, as from now on, definitely, permanently, as the right without which there can be no others. We will associate ourselves for all time with those who agree to join us in that task.

Having firmly established that right, we will confer as to how much of other rights may be built upon it. As to this ownership of Empire business, we are prepared to say now that it belongs as much to any who will join us in the defence of that first and fundamental right, as to ourselves; that if there is any benefit of ownership, it belongs as much to those who will join us in resistance to war, as it does to us. Its trade, its development, its government, will be as much theirs, as ours.

Is all that very difficult? Would either the Smiths or Schmidts fail to understand it?

To say that this has been our purpose and policy all along is simply to be unaware of what we have been doing in the past. By word and deed—the word of our eminent politicians, Cabinet Ministers, commentators, writers, editors, ambassadors, public men—not merely have we denied

that we have any obligation to defend the victims
of aggression, but we have gone on learnedly to
explain that on no account should that obligation
be assumed; that to assume it meant war. And on
the economic side, far from declaring that our
Empire in so far as it can be called an Empire,
belongs to the world—first of all to those who live
in it, and then to those who would trade with it
—we have for a generation pursued a policy of
ever-increasing restriction, preferences, monopolies. The disadvantages which foreigners suffered
from our increasing tendency to monopoly, to
favouritism, to preferences have steadily increased. Tighter and tighter closed the doors
against men, as well as goods. Even when, under
a storm of terror, men fled from the concentration
camp, from torture, death, persecution, unname-
able and unbelievable, even then did we close the
doors, admitting tens when—to our very great advantage—we could and should have admitted
thousands. And those to whom we thus refused
sanctuary are precisely those whom we now ask to
be our allies, within the borders not merely of
Bohemia, Slovakia, of Austria, of Poland, but of
Germany itself. The very children of the men who
embraced the cause of freedom were those whom
the nations of the Empire, including the great
empty countries, refused to receive.

Perhaps we shall have no case unless we can

make it clear that that conception of "right" is at an end, that those who will defend with us our heritage will also have the right to share it.

NOTE

The preceding paragraph has reference to the refugee policy recently pursued by Britain and other nations of the Commonwealth (as well as by the United States).

We have, of course, to-day allies, an army, within the German Reich itself—those who desire to see the overthrow of the regime which we fight. That army consists not only of the Czechs and Austrians, but of hundreds of thousands of German Social-Democrats, Catholics, Protestants, Jews.

Many of these allies of ours want to find a refuge for their women and children. For, of course, it is part of the Nazi technique to get at a man by threatening his wife and children. Many fighting the battle of freedom in Germany face this sort of problem. "We are ready to die for our convictions. But are we justified in making our children, our womenfolk suffer still worse tortures for them?" Many an anti-Nazi has said: "If I can find a refuge for the wife and children I will stick it out. If I cannot I must yield."

In the light of that recall the sort of thing you may read any day in the Press: Refugees picked up at sea from some crazy cockleshell in which they had hoped to escape, and sent back to the prison and the torture house—sent back by democracies;

the dependents of the very soldiers fighting our cause handed over to the mercies of the enemy; women strapped to the seats of the train or 'plane, in order that they should not destroy themselves on England's free soil; shiploads of women and children sailing the seas, finding no refuge anywhere. Even America has caught this fatal moral infection. One of these wandering refugee ships tried—quite unsuccessfully—to secure entrance for a few of the victims in an American port. It passed near the Statue of Liberty, and someone might have told them what was written, in a generation better than ours, upon its pedestal. This is written:

Give me your tired, your poor,
Your huddled masses yearning to be free,
The wretched refuse of your teeming shore.
Send these, the homeless, tempest tost, to me,
I lift my lamp beside the golden door.

But the children of the soldiers of freedom, fleeing from death, found it to be a closed door, like ours, with the lamp gone out. All the doors, whatever the democratic flag that flew over them, were closed; all the lamps were going out. Though the mothers asked nothing better than to scrub floors or wash dishes for any pittance that would give their babies food, that pittance, that food, that sanctuary again and again we have refused. We fear that the children might prove to be children of the race of Jesus and of Mary, and we urge that the presence of children of His and Her race might "excite prejudice," would make some of us angry. And the cost of their food might increase the taxes, though by an individual contribution so small that it cannot be calculated. So we turn these children, and their mothers, back to hunger and imprisonment, torture, death.

"Inasmuch as . . ."

If that is the degree of unity which marks "the forces of freedom throughout the world," if that the degree of faith in the principle that we must stand together against the forces of evil; if we believe the words that we are members one of another with that degree of fervour—then our material power obviously cannot save us. For we have not the moral unity sufficient to mobilize it and to use it; it can be overcome by those who have less power but greater unity. And our democracies would perish.

Perhaps they would deserve to perish, for they would be little better than the enemies they fought.

CHAPTER IX

WHAT SHOULD BE BRITAIN'S IDEOLOGY?

We are apt to argue that because ideologies and creeds lead to war it is better to have none. It is a false conclusion. It is true that religions have led to war; but it is also true that men may have religions without going to war; and if we enter a war without a sound creed we are likely to come out of it with a false one. And our own creed cannot be a sound one, nor prevail over the enemy's, unless we see clearly why his is wrong and ours is right. What is there in his creed that attracts him? Our ideology should be rooted in a feeling for the constitutional principle of common resistance to violence, to bullying; in a sense of the need for defending that principle as the basis of civilization.

To SAY that we need an ideology or a creed is merely, of course, another way of saying that we need to have an aim, to know what we are fighting for.

The enemy has his. It may be an utterly wrong and false creed, but it is one appealing to many of the fiercest instincts and most deeply-ingrained weaknesses of men, and by the younger generations at least is held with fanatical conviction.

The indoctrination, the conditioning of the

youth is carried out with scientific thoroughness, by methods of applied psychology, cunningly devised to excite deep feeling. It is made understandable—understandable, it is true, in terms of monstrous fallacies, of assumptions which flatter vanity, sadism, all the weaknesses of our imperfect human nature. But it is understood by the simplest, especially when it comes to foreign policy. Thus, it says in effect to the youth of Germany:

You young Germans belong to the noblest and greatest race ever born. You are surrounded for the most part by mongrels, ill disciplined, disorderly, ignoble. Your nation is an island in the midst of surrounding chaos and disorder. You must share that chaos or dominate it. It is your duty to dominate it, to rule this savagery, to bring order into it by virtue of the great qualities of rule which belong to your race. You need living space, the means of life, survival, that which is sought by every living creature. And through all nature there is one rule of survival which alone prevails—the strong demonstrate their worth, their superiority, their right to survive by overcoming the weak, ruling them; in the end for their good. It is the process by which the fit and noble survive over the meaner elements; by which the race becomes a race of strong and noble men, instead of weaklings.

The German race, the noblest race of all, has never sufficiently asserted its right to adequate living space. Others, even little nations, some of them mongrel nations, have expanded into the new world, into the depths of Africa, into the ancient world of Asia. Not one square yard in all that vast territory does Germany now possess. By what rule of equity is a dying race like the French, the Portuguese even, permitted vast territories throughout the world, while Germany must not hold one square yard?

Do you really think that this is a just and fair division of the world's wealth and resources, that *our* race should be doomed to poverty and scarcity, while nations that cannot even people and colonize their own countries should thus be permitted to squander vast wealth they can never fitly use?

That monstrous inequity has arisen because Germans, considerate, loving peace, knowledge, philosophy, science, music and art, have allowed themselves to be elbowed out by inferior but more acquisitive and avaricious peoples. To continue this is to betray our nation, our posterity; to surrender the rights due to us; to forgo all that Germany is and might be. That is why you were born perhaps to die for Germany.[1]

This is the sort of creed with which young Germany is so thoroughly indoctrinated. It contains numberless fallacies. But those fallacies are not apparent to those to whom the creed is taught.

[1] For development of this theme see the author's *Peace with the Dictators?*, particularly the first chapter entitled "The German Speaks."

Are they apparent to us, to neutrals, to those who should be on our side?

The answer is that we and the world share in large part the fallacies about survival through preponderant power, about the struggle of armed nations being, in fact, a struggle for bread, for a fair share in the wealth of the world, for existence. This Nazi view about the present maldistribution of the world's wealth is a view which seems to nearly everyone an obviously true view.

This picture of John Bull, as a fat, overfed, rich owner of a large part of the earth, owning it to the exclusion of others just as deserving; the view that our Empire is an estate which we "own," deriving great wealth and benefit therefrom—is a view held not alone by Germans, Americans, neutrals. It is a view held by our own Conservatives, and by crusaders like those who have for years propounded the political theories of the Beaverbrook Press, who want to continue to own, and draw wealth from it. The view that we "own" the Empire is shared by the Left, who want to bring the ownership, the imperialism and exploitation to an end. Right and Left alike are thus in agreement that the ownership is real, that the term is no misnomer. Right and Left alike thus grant by implication, as we shall see later in these pages,[2] a large part of the Nazi economic premises.

[2] Chapter XIV.

It is not surprising, therefore, that if so much of it seems reasonable to us, it all seems reasonable to the Nazi. Certain questions arise.

Have we any explainable creed, *weltanschauung*, theory of international life, of the universe, wherewith to support our case, our view, which is equally explainable, equally simple, which two out of any three men in the street, chosen at hazard, could propound as readily as the average Nazi youngster can propound *his* basic principles?

To that question, if we are honest, we shall answer no.

Now, if of two contending parties, one has a passionate, fanatical, Mohammedan-like faith in his cause, and the other has no particular faith, is doubtful as to what his cause is, and stands for —which of the two is likely to have the stiffer morale?

One would assume the answer to be that the advantage and morale would be with those who have a faith and an ideal, however mistaken, so long as it is sincere.

But the answer which many of us have been giving for years is that we ought not to have a political faith at all, for that would be an "ideology." And at all costs, we have been repeating, must we avoid "ideologies." "No war of ideologies." Repeatedly we have been warned against drifting into "a war of ideologies." Ideology is anathema. We must not really believe in anything.

It is easy to see how that stage of moral nihilism, the belief that we must have no beliefs, has arisen.

Men have often gone to war for their beliefs, their convictions, usually false beliefs, erroneous convictions. Therefore, if you want to avoid war you must shed belief, faith, conviction, or you will run into new wars, wars of religion in one form or another.

It is a fallacious conclusion. The right alternative to drifting into war because your creed is a false one, is not to have no creed at all, but to see that it is a sound one; that is a creed out of which will grow a system of order that will give the greatest chance of eliminating war.

It is true that we are confronted by the danger of rival religions: Communist, Socialist, Marxist, on the one side, Fascist, Nazi, Capitalist, *bourgeois*, on the other. It is true that the fiercest wars of the past have sometimes been wars of religion. But it is also true that men can manage to hold different religions without going to war about it; for they have done it. The wars of religion in the old sense have ceased. It is for us now to do for the political and social faiths what we have already done for the religious faiths.

Since, when we speak of the danger of a war of

ideologies we usually have in mind wars arising out of the "class conflict," one of the first questions we have to answer is whether there is a principle for which socialists on the one side and capitalists or *bourgeois* or Fascists (or however the opponents of Socialism would now be classed) on the other can stand in common. Is there some political principle common to the interests of both?

Now it is one of the ironies of the present situation that the affirmative answer to that question has been given most resoundingly, most emphatically, not only in words but deeds, by, of all people, Stalin, speaking for, of all nations, Soviet Russia, on the one side, and by Hitler and Nazi Germany on the other. The very archangels of Marxism have, by what they have done, declared that a Communist State can have a common purpose, a political purpose, with the fiercest and most ruthless of capitalist states (for most Marxists have heretofore insisted that Nazism is just an effort of capitalism to preserve its threatened dominance). That common purpose is of course self-preservation. No such arrangement as that which has just been made between Russia and Germany could possibly have been concluded on any other basis than by each agreeing: "If you will respect our freedom to manage our state as seems best to us, we will respect your freedom to manage your state as seems best to you. This implies by its very terms absence of aggression, the one upon the other."

It is surely most illuminating that these two states of all states, both "dynamic," "expansionist," in their respective ways, have been forced to abandon reciprocal aggression in their relations with each other and to adopt this principle of co-operating with a hostile "religion" for achieving the one purpose common to both: security; have been forced to such co-operation despite years of passionate protestations that no such co-operation could ever be possible. Hardly less illuminating is the fact that on our side, too, a government which, with its supporters, had for years disparaged and derided a given principle of foreign policy, which is also a principle of security, have been forced, suddenly, to adopt that heretofore derided principle.

§

I am suggesting that there is revealed here a principle of policy—however little we may have perceived its nature, and however little we may perceive it to-day—so vital to civilization and order of any kind, Socialist, Communist, Capitalist, *Bourgeois*, that it will when perceived override all other doctrinal differences; and that upon that principle we should build our ideology, our creed. It should not be a merely national creed because we desire that it should be shared as much as possible by France, by America, by all nations. But it can be national in the sense that the whole nation, irrespective of "class-war" or other conflict, holds it, and holds it in part because without it nationality itself is not safe.

It has not been our creed heretofore, it has indeed usually been disparaged because we simply have not perceived with any vividness the nature of this principle, its indispensability; have not fully realized how much it is the core, the foundation of all our securities.

A definition of that principle and a sketch of the way in which it forms the basis of all orderly society, was attempted in the previous chapter. It was there defined as the common defence of the right of each to existence, the right of each member of a society, whether that member be nation or person, to protection from violence, from killing, from extinction; or from the threat of those things as the only alternative to another's lawless will. Within the state this right is expressed as "the protection of the Law" or the Constitutional Principle. Force as the instrument of rival parties within the state, one armed party confronting another, would soon bring utter anarchy, chaos, extinction of all law or right. But force as the instrument of the constitution defending any individual or group the victim of violence

—a political party attacked by some other party, a trade union attacked by armed bullies, a church the victim of some Ku-Klux-Klan—becomes, however paradoxical at first glance, an instrument for the elimination of force and violence.

It has been Britain's genius in the past to recognize that "force belongs to the constitution alone," to have a sure instinct that in "common defence of the constitution" (even when no one quite knew what the constitution was) lay the secret of order and freedom. Not all national societies have been quite so clear as to the proper function of force. In Spain, in Spanish America, and recently in nations infected with Fascism, conceptions are much more confused as to the proper place of force. "If one party, that of the government, can use force to keep its power, then other parties are entitled to use it to take power."

It is out of such confusion that have arisen the revolutions, chaos, anarchy, of which the end is not yet.

Cannot Britain now make of the defence of this "constitutional principle," in international affairs, the principle that in our human society violence shall be resisted as such, not only the keystone of her foreign policy but truly her creed, her "ideology" in all that relates to her contacts with others?

If there has not been much feeling for it in the

past, it is because as soon as it is proposed to make that principle the basis of our own defence, all those strange confusions ("Why should we fight for Abyssinia?"—"You can't make peace by threatening war") outlined in previous chapters and discussed more freely in later chapters, begin to paralyse our will.

§

The failure of our victory of 1918 to achieve the results which had been hoped for it, has been assigned to many causes, some of which are examined in the pages that follow.

But it is at this point suggested that there is one ultimate cause—this:

While men are ready to defend their own nation, and make sacrifices for its safety, to fight and die for it, they have not been willing to defend, and to fight for the general security of international society, the law under which others may have security as well as themselves, for the principle of security as such.

The intention behind this refusal has usually been good, usually the hatred of war, the desire to avoid mixing in the quarrels of others, "strange people of whom we know nothing," a desire for peace. It seemed to most men to reduce the effort for peace to utter absurdity to suggest that it would be saved by "threatening others with war because we did not like their behaviour."

(Though that is precisely what we do under the old method of defence.)

Out of this confusion—for confusion it is, however good the motive behind it—that while it is right for each in the family of nations to defend himself, it is wrong for the whole family to defend each—has arisen an indecision, an oscillation of purpose which ended by defeating the purposes for which the last war was waged.

It may be utterly wrong to go to war at all, to kill and torture millions of innocent people, including little children, for some political difference—the difference between, say, the Nazi form of dictatorship, or the liberal democratic form. No one, capable of serious thought, would ever treat that proposition with anything but respect. But it cannot be right to do those dreadful things whenever we deem our own security or interests or possessions endangered or attacked, and wrong to do them when the attack is merely against others, the general interest, the law or principle which generally maintained would make war impossible.

There is here a complete moral inversion. For each to say, "I will defend myself, myself and my interests only, by being stronger than any nation who might challenge me," is to assert a principle which generally followed must on the face of it make war inevitable. For each claims the right to be stronger than the other, each the "right" to have power of judgment over the other, each side, that is to say, claims "rights" it denies to the other. Such claims are the negation of Right.

But if each says: "We will defend any member who is made the victim of violence, of war; an attack on one is an attack on all, and will extend that right of defence equally to each," there is erected a general rule reducing the chances of attack, of war, to the very minimum. That principle is indeed the basis of all organized society, for it ensures that force shall be used in the most effective, the least evil way, for the purpose which is the most fundamental of all purposes of living things—self-preservation, survival. Unless that primary need of defence, survival, is ensured by the defence of a general rule against violence, there can be no order and no civilization.

In attempting to explain the conduct of men, and nations; to determine what motives run deepest, we shall not go far wrong if we search, first of all, for that instinct or motive which animates every living thing—the impulse to self-preservation, to survival. How have states in the past used force as an instrument of that purpose of self-preservation in their relations with others? And what has been the result?

The familiar, the approved method, not merely of the past, but of to-day still, with the immense majority of states, is that each seeks the maximum of power for himself in order to be his own defender, supplemented, as needs arise, by temporary *ad hoc* arrangements with others when their immediate interests happen to coincide.

But power is a relative thing. You are strong with two ships if your enemy has only one; weak with two hundred if he has three hundred. And if you can look to no source of aid except your own strength, you must, of course, be stronger than any potential enemy in order to have secure defence. But in that case, what becomes of *his* defence? By that method the two can only be really defended when again each is stronger than the other. The difficulty is moral as well as arithmetical. If we say we have the right to defence, survival, self-preservation, and therefore the right to be stronger, then we deny to the other the same right of defence by superior power we claim for ourselves.

It goes deeper. Defence does not, cannot be a mere defence of the national soil. We have had numberless wars since 1066, not one fought against a foreign enemy on our soil since that date. In fighting in every country of the world we were defending not our soil, but interests, rights, sustaining our view of our rights when others challenged our rights, anywhere in the world.

When, therefore, we say that we have the right to be stronger in order to defend our vital interests, what we really mean is that when we differ with others as to what our rights are, when it is a question of which of us is right, we are claiming that we must be in such a position (that is to say stronger) as to be the sole judge of that question.

In other words, by demanding preponderance of power, not for a law which we offer to the other party and by which we ourselves are prepared to abide but preponderance for ourselves, "our side" we claim not merely the right to defence by superior power denied to the other, but also a right of judgment between us which we deny to him.

Now this is not just a logician's artificial dilemma. It is the tragic dilemma of all European history. The conflict with Germany in 1914 illustrated it vividly. Seeing the possibility that if France and Russia were beaten by Germany we should be in a position of such inferiority of power as to be unable to defend our rights, we said in effect: "No free country can accept such a position of defencelessness and be at the mercy of another."

So far we were right. Czecho-Slovakia, Poland,

illustrate what happens to countries that become inferior in power to their neighbours.

What was our alternative, however, to refusal to accept the preponderance of Germany's power in 1914? The alternative we suggested was in effect that she should accept our preponderance. To prove to her that she could do so safely we made the Treaty of Versailles. Looking at to-day the Germans say: "That is what comes of being weaker than your potential enemy. You never get justice. To get justice you must be stronger." She has proceeded to make herself stronger, and during the last year or two has been so strong as to be able to tear up completely the Treaty of Versailles.

If she should win this war she will write a Treaty of Versailles differing greatly from the one we wrote. It will not be better or milder. It will be immensely more unjust.

In the presence of it, what shall we do, even if we lose this particular war? We shall do what the Germans have been doing: build up our power, make greater concessions to Russia or others, threaten war, finally beat Germany once more, and summon her once more to Versailles, and make a new treaty as much worse than the one we wrote in 1919, as there are more wrongs to avenge. And if the Germans rebelled against the Treaty of 1919, they will have still greater cause to rebel against the new one. New war for new treaty. . . .

Again, all that is not some effort of imagination as to how things might turn out. It is an outline sketch of precisely what has been unrolling in political and military fact beneath our noses.

It has happened, not because the German people are more wicked than others (the Germany that went to war in 1914 was a relatively liberal state with a large socialist party, parliamentary institutions, and not a single concentration camp in the whole of the Reich); not even because of the peculiar moral character of the Kaiser, who was not more of an autocrat than the Tsar, who became our ally; nor even because Hitler is, after all, any worse than Turkish sultans who betimes were also our allies, nor, for that matter, responsible for devastation and misery anything like as great as that inflicted by Japan on China, or worse than that inflicted by Mussolini on Abyssinians and Spaniards.

The evil dilemma we have faced all these years was not made by Hitler, evil as he is. It results from the method of defence followed by all nations alike, a method of so using force for self-preservation that it is bound to defeat its purpose, because it is a method under which the security of one is purchased at the price of the insecurity of another; because the "rights" claimed by one party could only be granted by denying similar rights to the other. So long as our method of defence is thus based upon defiance of arithmetic, the attempt, that is, of each to be stronger than the other, and defiance of right through denial to some other of the judgment we claim for ourselves, and so long as each disregards the truth that in order to defend ourselves we must of necessity defend others, then the results we now see will continue to be produced. The dilemma cannot be dodged by such devices as Balance of Power by "parity of armaments," a parity depending upon balancing industrial resources against armed forces, coaling stations against ships, strategic position against mechanization, so that no one can tell when we have reached a balance; a parity which can be upset by such a diplomatic move as the recent one of Russia, a move which shifted over power from our side to the enemy's from one day to another.

The real case for the policy which Hitler (or Russia) has followed resides in this: that given a condition of international anarchy, the only alternative to dominating others is the risk of being dominated by them. Hitler has explained again and again in all that he says and writes that his supreme purpose is to make sure that never again shall Germany find herself at the mercy of a combination of her neighbours. It simply will not do to explain to him that Britain is prepared to be

fair, that France has no desire for aggression.
Germany was assured before the war that British
power could never be used for injustice. Yet it
was British power that made the Treaty of Versailles, in the sense that without that power it
could never have been made. Britain has indeed
since explained that there are features in the
Versailles Treaty that she would have desired
otherwise, that were no part of her intention, that
they are there because of obligations to allies. But
she will have obligations again. Those obligations
inevitably arise when alliances of others have to
be purchased by promises of a share of the loot.

It is possible, of course, that Germany *might* be
secure in a political and economic sense if Russia,
Britain and Poland, Turkey, Roumania, Greece,
all combined against her, so that they constituted
a plain preponderance of power. They might use
that power well, admits Hitler by implication.
But then on the other hand they might not. Their
power would not be the instrument of any clear
code of right and obligation, applicable to all
alike, but would be "irresponsible" in the sense
that it would be exercised as the victors saw fit
at the moment, unrestrained by obligation to a
law to which they had subscribed. And just as
Britain will not allow any other nation to dominate the sea, because free use of the sea is indispensable to her life, and there is no "freedom of

the seas," which nations are clearly pledged to
support, so Germany cannot afford to see a combination dominate the land, a certain freedom of
access to which in the shape of markets as a means
of buying food is indispensable to her. Germany
is merely applying with thorough German logic,
the principle that she can never be safe so long as
others are in a position to dominate her by power,
the purpose of which is not only unknown, which
not only stands for no code that even promises
Germany protection, but is a force held by those
who have declared repeatedly that a commonly
defended international code is a wrong principle.
The repudiation of the collective principle so fre-
quent in British opinion of recent years, so em-
phatic, often so strident, has merely been a
notification to Germany that she must accept our
domination, unless she can compel us to accept
hers.

Now this conflict of power in that way is no new
story. It is all part of an ancient and obstinate
dilemma in human relationship. When it arose,
not merely in respect of the security of one nation
as against another, but in respect of the rights of
groups or parties within a nation—rival chieftains,
rival political parties, rival religions—in the end
only one way out has been found.

That way has not been by surrendering defence,

by abolishing force, by what is to-day known as the pacifist solution.

Nor have we found a way out by general promises of good behaviour, by the redress of specific grievances (Germany had no grievances against us in 1914, and we had none against her except the supreme grievance that her victory would deprive us of defence). The way out of this dilemma, whether it arose as between parties or corporate bodies within the state, or between states, has been a process of what I have described as increasing power behind the constitutional principle, increasing transfer of force from the litigant to the law, from parties or groups within a state to the constitution.

In the case of nations, that law in its first form, need only be a very simple one: There shall be no more war. The purpose of force shall be to prevent force being used, as our state would prevent an armed Fascist Party coercing a Liberal or Communist party, or vice versa; by ensuring defence of the victim of violence wherever violence is used. Effective law and effective constitutionalism, the ending of anarchy, the building up of a workable society, are all rooted in this one principle—the collective defence of the members or units who form that society. This principle truly is not the whole of law; it is its foundation.

It is not of itself enough. It is merely indispensable.

This surely is not a very complicated principle. Yet, again, infinite confusions seem to grow up around it as anyone who has listened to dinner-table or public-house conversation can quite certainly discover for himself. "What in Heaven's name," say equally the Cabinet Minister and the bricklayer, "have we to do with these Czechs or Slovaks or whatever they call themselves? Let them settle their own troubles. They are certainly no concern of ours."

Powerful newspaper campaigns, whether waged by a Hearst syndicate in America, or a Beaverbrook syndicate in Britain, sustain huge circulation by a constant appeal to this moral ignorance, this ethical illiteracy. They—with many others—carry on their crusades because, as good journalists, they are aware that such appeals respond to a very ancient prejudice, and a very deep impulse, in human beings; the impulse to have as little as possible to do with foreigners, and the impulse, if we have to treat with them, to do so from a position of domination; to be their masters, and refuse all partnership with them.

These campaigns have of late years been helped by those who most desire peace, the most pacifically minded, as well as by those who are not pacifically minded at all, but are passionately nationalist; who, ready enough to fight for Britain, refuse to fight for the law, for the constitution, for "foreigners." While Pacifists have opposed defence of the Covenant because such defence might involve war, Nationalists have opposed it because it implies internationalism.

In opposition to the principle which Britain now proclaims, as that for which we are fighting, we have had for years within Britain a combination of the most pacifically minded and most military minded. It is a powerful combination.

Between the two extremes there has been fatal indecision and confusion of purpose. When abandonment of the law, the Covenant, seemed to ensure peace, for the time being, many favoured that course, later to discover that it was not merely peace they wanted. They also wanted defence, security. And when, as a result of repeated abandonment of the constitutional principle, the peril to ourselves was obviously mortal, they forgot their pacifism, and suddenly made a stand, as in the diplomatic revolution of March last. And war was precipitated.

In this oscillation, we see on one swing of the pendulum, nations pursue peace for themselves irrespective of what happens to others, demand freedom from foreign commitments, repudiation of all obligation to support any general law against war, any constitutional principle or covenant.

Then when that course has produced its inevitable results of endangering defence, there is formed a hurried defensive combination against the now obvious threat. That sort of oscillation is not merely the story of the sudden engagement of the whole world in war in 1914-18, arising out of an attack on a little state in the Balkans; of America's sudden abandonment of isolation, and entrance into that war, and then afterwards her equally sudden return to isolation; of Britain's "war for Belgium," and after it the refusal for more than a decade to guarantee even France; and then a sudden guarantee to states on the other side of Europe; not merely the story of the refusal to stand by Manchuria, or China, or Abyssinia, or Spain, when the risk would have been small; followed by plunging into war for the defence of Poland; it is the story of Europe ever since nationality and nationalism became the basis of its political structure. How long is the story to continue?

Is the next episode to repeat the former ones, the new victory to be as worthless as the last?

The general effect of the new type of pacifism was to implant, as we now know, in the minds of those who desired conquests, the conviction that aggression was a safe policy; that it would encounter nothing in the way of collective resistance. And there duly followed a long list of aggressions

—Manchuria, giving rise to Abyssinia, Abyssinia in its turn convincing Hitler that he could occupy the Rhineland without opposition. Having proved it, he went on to the occupation of Austria, the invasion of Spain; thence to the claims on Czecho-Slovakia, the acquisition of Memel, of Bohemia, Moravia, Poland. Italy, meantime, following the seizure of Abyssinia by the seizure of Albania, threats to, and demands on France—"Tunis, Corsica, Savoy."

Throughout, the French and British governments justified their acquiescence in this long series of aggressions by a pacifist appeal, by turning round to the public and saying in effect: "Do you want war?" And that pacifist appeal satisfied the national conscience. It was an effort to avoid war: that justified it. Those who criticized, entered any caveat, were often violently attacked as "war mongers," "war-mongering Geneva fists." The commonest statement was that if such critics (who, in the later stages included, it will be recalled, Mr. Churchill, Mr. Eden and Mr. Duff Cooper) had had their way we should have been involved in three wars: with Japan over Manchuria, with Italy over Abyssinia, and with Germany over Austria and the Sudetenland.

If this appeal had been made by pacifists who did not believe in armed defence at all, who

would not have fought for the defence even of
their own country, it would have been at least
morally consistent and intellectually respect-
worthy. But it was made by men, who, while refusing to take the risks of war in order to help
others to resist aggression, on behalf of the principle of law, insisted that war was entirely justifiable, if it were on behalf of our own direct
interests; if we ourselves were the victims of aggression. So long, it was argued, as the aggressors
confine their attack on others, we are not concerned. To use our power for the security of other
states was declared to be a foolish and mischie-
vous knight-errantry. A thousand times was it all
dismissed with such phrases as that "we could not
be the world's policeman." We should fight only
for certain very limited objectives: to repel attacks
on our own territory, on that of France, Belgium,
Egypt and Iraq. With the rest we were not concerned. Particularly were we to avoid any sort of
commitment in Eastern Europe. With what
energy, sometimes with what passion, we rejected
the principle that we had any interest or obligation in resistance to aggression as such some of
the evidence in these pages reveals.

In and out of season, many critics, of which this
writer was one, insisted that the policy we were
then pursuing, of acquiescing in aggression, and

as quickly as possible giving official recognition to its fruits (as we did in the case of Italy, with visits to Rome, by the Prime Minister and the Foreign Minister, and the accompaniment of flattering speeches and banquets) was suicidal; that to go on saying, "We don't care what you do to others, if only you don't do it to us," was as contemptible in morals as it was imbecile in politics; that we were acquiescing in a process of destroying potential allies in the only policy that could effectively defend us; that each successful aggression made resistance to the next aggression more difficult; that there would come a point at which as a matter of the most obvious self-preservation, we should have to stand on the principle, and that when we did so stand, we should find that the ground had been strategically undermined; that if we were to be compelled to stand for that principle late, it would reduce the risk of war if we stood for it early. Had we accepted, in 1932, before even the arrival of Hitlerism and the re-armament of Germany, Mr. Stimson's offer of co-operation in refusing recognition of Japan's conquests in China, associated ourselves completely with American policy in the matter, we certainly ran no risk of the destruction of London from the air. Had we, two years later, when Italian intentions about Abyssinia had become plain, said "We shall defend Abyssinia, that is to say, the principle of no war, exactly as we should defend Kenya," there would have been no war. (We know that if Abyssinia had been a British colony, it would never have been attacked, whatever the strength or weaknesses in the Mediterranean might at the moment have been.) We should no more have precipitated war by making clear that we should defend Abyssinia, than we precipitate war by making it clear that we should defend Malta or Iraq or Kent. The assumption that it is *not* war-mongering to announce our defence of Malta, or Gibraltar, because they are imperial possessions, part of the means by which we propose to dominate others, but *is* war-mongering to announce our defence of a Covenant which would give to others the same right of defence we claim, is indeed a strange topsy-turviness of thought.

It will be for the reader to judge whether the forecasts made so often that the continual surrenders of the law, and submission to those who violated it, would in the end precipitate war, have been justified by the event, or not; how far this war is due mainly to the belief in Hitler's mind that having got away with so many bloodless conquests, he should get away with yet another; his belief that the new undertakings to resist aggression would in the end prove little more real than all the previous undertakings which, put to the test, proved not to be real at all.

§

Came the great diplomatic revolution of March 1939. All the arguments that the road to peace was not by defending the law as such, but by bargains with the violator when it was broken; all the arguments about having no interest in the frontiers of Eastern Europe; all our repudiations and derisions of the principle that "peace is indivisible"—all this, as we know, was suddenly abandoned almost from one day to another, in a change of foreign policy which the world has agreed to regard as one of the most amazing diplomatic revolutions of modern history. What at the beginning of March was dangerous, war engendering "Midsummer Madness," had, by the end of March, become the eternal principle inspiring all British foreign policy, to be defended by all that we had and were.

Why must all this be recalled? In part because the world that knows or cares anything at all of foreign affairs recalls it; because all intelligent America recalls it, and wants to know our attitude towards it all; wants to know whether we perceive the defects of our past policy or are still blind to them. If it is clear that we remain blind, they—those who might be associated with us, now or

later, in making a safer world—will be extremely
chary of any such association. For they will con-
clude inevitably that such blindness means we do
not learn, are impervious to experience, to the
lesson of fact; and that, therefore, our conduct or
policy is likely to be in the future what it has been
in the past, producing for them, if they should be
foolish enough to become associated with us, the
same disastrous results which our past policy has
produced for ourselves.

Unless we understand the forces which produced this diplomatic revolution of March, it will
be no more permanent than previous phases of
foreign policy have been. Nor without such understanding can we hope to understand, nor make
others understand, what we are fighting for, what
our aims are supposed to be; nor come to the
peace table with any better grasp of how our purpose of a Europe free from aggression is to be
made any more effective.

§

Any attempt to disentangle a few guiding principles from the complexity of detail is apt to
encounter the objection that merely to understand
a general principle will not enable you to apply
it to practical life, to complicated political situations. You must understand the complications as
well as the principle.

That is perfectly true. When, however, the critic goes on to say something which sounds like it, but which is in fact entirely different, namely that until you are familiar with complications—the complexities of Balkan politics, the varying ethnographical claims of Eastern and South-Eastern Europe and what not—it serves no purpose to be familiar with general principles, he says something which is quite untrue. For while a sense of the underlying principle will not make it more difficult for you to understand the complexities (but will often indeed make it much easier, serving as a compass through the forest which the trees prevent you seeing), it will enable you also at least to avoid wrong solutions, piling up fresh difficulties. To know what we ought not to do is a help in finding out what we ought to do.

It is just because the non-expert public had *not* a clear vision of the underlying principle that again and again they have pushed their governments to do the wrong thing, the very thing sometimes which the experts do not wish them to do.

The follies of the reparations settlement were notably such a case. And even at Versailles the supreme error was to refuse discussion of the settlement to the Germans, making it thus truly a dictated peace, a verdict imposed by one of the parties to the dispute, one of the litigants upon the other, a verdict given when only one side had been able to present its case. Even a just verdict becomes in these circumstances unjust, as the little parables unfolded above try to indicate. Yet great experts in the politics of England and South-Eastern Europe, indeed most of the experts at Versailles, overlooked that fact, and where they did not overlook it were not able to carry their point, because public opinion was indifferent to it, and governments followed the line of least resistance.

But the public would have insisted upon an entirely different policy if they had applied to politics a truth which does not derive at all from specialist's knowledge of European politics, but from a clear perception of the very elementary social fact that whatever the intrinsic merit of the settlement, however just, this feature of dictation would be bound to upset it, and cause infinite trouble in the future.

The public took the contrary line, encouraged the governments to refuse to discuss with "Huns and murderers," and the disregard of so simple a piece of elementary knowledge made the learning of the experts of no avail.

Perception of similarly elementary truth will be necessary when we come to the economic aspect of the settlement which will confront us at the next peace-making. We must say to the Germans, to the world:

This Empire which you say we own, we do not own at all. In proof of that we now declare squarely that you can enter it and share it on exactly the same terms as ourselves. We shall sacrifice nothing in so doing. On the contrary we shall gain.

But to many millions of average English folk the proposition seems monstrous and outrageous on its face. They too believe that we really do own Canada and Australia and India and New Zealand, and the rest of it. They are, of course, hypnotized by words; form on the basis of those words this picture of John Bull, as the plutocratic landowner, which is discussed elsewhere in these pages. The facts which would destroy that picture are almost self-evident facts, or at least available to knowledge which is of universal possession. The common man of Sweden, Norway, Denmark, Switzerland, "owns" no Empire, but has a standard of life certainly as high as that of, and carries economic burdens very much less than the common man of Britain, who "owns" half a universe. That is the broad truth, however the learned may qualify and complicate it. The realization of that truth would encourage the innate generosity and good will of the common man, encourage him to offer to the world to come in and share our heritage.

If that too were part of our creed, and on the basis of that faith, we made a generous offer to

the world in terms so simple that none could mis-
understand them, then indeed would the world
see that we stood on the economic as on the
political side, for principles which are truly social,
for a creed they could support.

But, alas! also by reason of miscomprehension
of certain very simple things we have of recent
years taken the entirely contrary line of shutting
others out from our Empire, of trying to monopo-
lize its trade and wealth.

CHAPTER X

THE UNLEARNED LESSONS

*The most elementary, as well as the most tragic lessons
of the war of 1914-18 relating to the way in which a lone
force may be made the instrument of order and peace, of
the constitutional principle, have not only been missed;
they have been turned upside down, even by the more
responsible leaders of public opinion. An honest stock-
taking and revision of opinion must be faced if the repetition of devastating error is to be avoided.*

A NUMBER of historians dealing with the war of
1914-18 have put the question: Could it have
been prevented? They have replied, "Yes," but on
one condition only, namely, that the Germans,
government and people alike, had been brought
fully to realize beforehand that the policy they
were following would finally have to meet the
resistance that it actually did have to meet.

That indeed is fairly self-evident. If it had been
plain to the Reich Government of 1912-13 that by
following their then line they would bring into
the field against them not merely France and
Russia and Belgium, but Britain, Italy, Japan,
Roumania, and finally the vast powers of the
United States; and a round dozen other states

associated with those as benevolently un-neutral neutrals, the Reich would not have followed that line, and—at the time at least—there would have been no war. Governments do not enter wars for the purpose of losing them, and such a war, confronting such power, was bound to be lost.

But the Germans had no knowledge, in the circumstances, could have had no such knowledge, that their policy would meet with that degree of resistance. No man living in 1910—or 1914, for that matter—could have foreseen that great American armies would cross the seas to fight in France beside the armies of that country, as well as the armies of Belgium, Portugal, India, Canada, New Zealand, men from the Arctic, from Newfoundland, Fiji.

Such a display of the power of the universe thus resisting aggression was magnificent. But it was not peace. Its victory did not bring peace, as the event proved. All that vast, magnificent array of power failed as a deterrent of aggression, for the childishly simple reason that the aggressor did not know he would have to meet it.

Now it is quite obvious that if you are proposing to make yourself strong in order to prevent someone doing certain things, that someone must know that he will have to meet your power and what the things are he must not do, otherwise your power cannot possibly have deterrent effect.

This writer has happened to have put the case in these terms: Had the relations of the allies before the war been such as to enable them to say beforehand that they *would* do, what finally they felt they were compelled to do, they would not have had to do it. In other words, the cause of the war was decision or statement too long deferred as to what we would regard as aggression, what we deemed necessary to our defence.

Note, however, that that statement, true as far as it goes, is incomplete, as we shall see presently; that though the knowledge that resistance would be made by that wide range of powers would have deterred aggression for the time being, the power itself would have broken down in the end unless certain other things were added—what things will be indicated in due course.

Even so, the reply is a tragic one when one reflects upon all that it embraces: ten million dead; ten million who had better have been dead; civilization in danger and the soul of man so injured that we have reverted to some of the most evil ferocities of the Dark Ages; the freedoms and accomplishments of the human spirit which we believed to be achieved for all time engulfed in hurricanes of terror and cruelty. And none of it, say the historians, need ever have been if only aggressors and defenders alike had been clearer as to what was aggression and what was defence.

Mr. Lloyd George, again like other historians, is most positive and categoric on these points. He declares that the Kaiser had not the remotest idea that the line he was taking would be regarded by other European States as an attack upon them of a kind that would provoke their armed resistance. Mr. Lloyd George's words are these:

I am convinced after a careful perusal of all the documents available on all sides that the Kaiser never had the remotest idea that he was plunging —or being plunged—into a European war. His first bluff of Russia over a Balkan question had been a triumphant success and had added a great deal to his prestige as the War Lord of Europe. He never doubted that he would score another success by the mere threat of war and thus establish still more firmly his diplomatic mastery over the Continent. After giving Austria that assurance of his support he left the bullying of Serbia in her hands. Serbia had dared to assassinate a future Emperor and deserved to be scourged. But it was too paltry a task for him to attend to the details of the lashing, so he went off on a sea cruise beyond the reach of urgent despatches without taking any thought of what preparations would be necessary to carry Germany through a great war. He was not anticipating a costly war but a cheap diplomatic triumph. When the Serbian reply was received, he thought it was satisfactory and that Austria ought to accept it. His Chancellor was opposed to war. His Foreign

Minister left Berlin on a honeymoon. The Chief of his Staff, von Moltke, was taking a cure at one of the German watering-places. The German public did not expect war—not even after they found their young men being called to the colours and entraining towards the frontiers. Had it been made clear in time to the Kaiser that Britain would make war upon Germany, if she invaded Belgium, he and his advisers would have paused to confer ere it became too late to withdraw. He had not accumulated sufficient stores of food or raw materials to face the blockade of the British Fleet. A halt of a few weeks to confer would have taken the nations near to the winter months when the march of gigantic armies would have been impeded in the West and impossible in the East. Mobilization had begun in Austria, Russia, France and Germany, and war had actually been declared between these Powers before Britain delivered her ultimatum about Belgium. It was then too late to recall the legions who were already hurrying to battle.

Every word of the foregoing passage ought to be studied carefully in the light of the drift of policy in Europe during the last seven or eight years.

For it means this. Not merely did the potential aggressor not know what others would regard as an attack. These others did not themselves know.

"No sovereign or leading statesman in any of the belligerent countries sought or desired war—

certainly not a European war," insists Mr. Lloyd
George. The Austrian Foreign Minister wanted
a punitive expedition against Serbia. Had he realized that it would involve war with Russia, Italy
and Roumania, supported by Britain, France, and
ultimately America, he would have modified the
terms of the ultimatum or accepted Serbia's answer, which was abject enough to satisfy even
Austrian pride. But he was convinced that Russia
would not face war with Germany. The Tsar had
retreated over the much more important question
of the annexation of Bosnia without striking a
blow. His army now was not much better prepared than it had been then. On the other hand,
Germany had considerably strengthened hers. So
the moment the Kaiser gave his word that he
would back up Austria's demands, Berchtold had
no doubt that Russia would give in and, if Serbia
were still obdurate, war with her would be a small
matter. What about Germany?

"France shrank from war, and there was nothing further from the mind of Britain or her Government at the end of July 1914, than the staging
of a Continental war. The negotiations were
botched by everybody engaged in directing them.
It is incredible that so momentous an issue should
have been handled in so unbusinesslike and casual
a manner. When a collision seemed inevitable
engine-drivers and signalmen lost their heads and

pulled the wrong levers. The stokers alone did their work. In politics one is accustomed to haphazard methods which produce minor disasters that overturn ministries. But this was a question of life and death for Empires, Kingdoms and Republics—and for millions of their subjects."[1]

One would have supposed that the lesson—the lesson, that if your power is to deter aggression, the aggressor must know that he will have to face it, that its purpose must be known, and its use predictable—which is so abundantly illustrated by experience, which is rooted in a truth so obvious as to be almost a truism, would be about the first political lesson to be definitely and permanently learned. It was about the first to be repudiated or forgotten.

Even before the peace was signed, and Foch was proposing fantastic settlements like the permanent occupation of the Rhineland, or the creation of an independent buffer state out of the Rhineland, we began to miss the whole point of this lesson. Some of the statesmen involved did at least see that you could not either permanently break up or permanently crush a nation of sixty or seventy million folk. "Very well," in effect said Foch, when this was pointed out, "then give us a permanent guarantee against her aggression; a

[1] *War Memoirs of David Lloyd George.* (Ivor, Nicholson & Watson.) Vol. VI, p. 3,346.

permanent guarantee for the defence of France."
And that was the demand presented by France as
the condition of lenient treatment of Germany.
Wilson and Lloyd George agreed. France was to
have a double guarantee of the United States and
Great Britain as the alternative to a policy of
crushing Germany.

We recall what happened. The American promise of the guarantee was not fulfilled. The British
promise was not fulfilled. Public opinion in both
countries made the fulfilment of the promise impossible. Not until seventeen years later did
Britain give at long last the unequivocal guarantee
for which France began asking in 1919.

Not getting the guarantee, France turned to the
alternative policy of weakening Germany, and
pursued it by every possible means; means which
included a relentless Reparations policy, an in-
cident of it being the invasion of the Ruhr; a
policy which helped to produce the inflation that
was the main element in the destruction of the
Weimar Republic, and the final arrival of Hitler.

The proposal to give the guarantees to France
was for years regarded as an anti-German policy;
addition to France's strength was regarded as
provocation for Germany. The road to peace it was
argued, was not to pile up anti-German power
but to redress Germany's grievances, and revise as
far as possible the bad features of the Versailles

Treaty. A false antithesis was thus created. Revision was regarded as the alternative to the collective system, already beginning to be regarded as a false policy of "preserving peace by threatening war."

It seemed impossible to get acceptance of the view that revision was not and could not be the alternative to guarantee, but that such security was the necessary condition for bringing revision and conciliation into effect. Again and again the best French minds presented the argument: "We will be as generous as you like to Germany provided that you will provide some sort of guarantee, collective or other, against the misuse of the power which Germany will acquire as the result of such generous treatment." But no. We seemed to oscillate between a muddled preference for the Balance of Power, half fearing that a German preponderance might be followed by a French, and a policy of general disarmament all round. In the absence of guarantee, France refused to disarm, or seriously reduce her armament.

We complained at the time that "France was always wanting us to fight for her." Which, of course, was the last thing that France wanted. She had had enough of wars on her soil. She wanted us to say that we would fight in given circumstances to the end that no fighting would be necessary. But to say this beforehand was a "dangerous commitment," constituted a military alliance. And all knew such alliances to be dangerous.

We argued—quite rightly—that to undertake beforehand to fight for another country might make us the victim of that country's bad foreign policy. The point was a perfectly sound one (it was made by Sir John Simon as late as March 1939, a few days before the guarantee was given to Poland when he said that the method of collective defence placed your foreign policy in "the hands of a lot of foreign governments").

But the right way to meet that perfectly sound objection was not to abandon the method of mutual guarantees, but to make the guarantee subject to some test of good political behaviour, an unaggressive policy on the part of the ally, the government to which the guarantee was extended.

The present writer recalls a conversation which he had with a certain French Prime Minister just before the latter was to confer with a British one. "Will your Government at long last," he said, "make it clear that if the Boche attacks once more he will have to meet your power as well as ours?"

I pointed out that we could not give a blanket guarantee to defend France whatever her policy: she might be so provocative as to make attack upon her certain, and we should be dragged into war in support of indefensible conduct.

He replied: "We are prepared to give you guarantees of good political behaviour, namely, an undertaking to submit any quarrel we may have with the Boche to third party judgment and only on his refusal to accept settlement on that basis to ask your aid." Even so I doubted whether Britain would, or should give such a guarantee unless the same guarantee could be extended to Germany herself. The Frenchman declared that France would accept that condition. But he entirely failed a little later to get any satisfactory agreement from Britain.

An attempt was made to give expression to that principle in a whole series of treaties. First as the result of the Herculean labour of Lord Cecil came the Treaty of Mutual Assistance. It failed of ratification as the earlier forms of guarantee to France had failed of ratification. There followed the Geneva Protocol; that too failed of ratification. The Locarno Treaties were actually signed and ratified. And no sooner had that taken place than there began a mass attack upon the whole underlying principle of collective resistance to aggression, an attack in which extreme Left and extreme Right joined hands.

§

At the beginning of this chapter it is suggested that one tragic fact about the last war is that it need never have taken place, and that a still more tragic one is that it failed in its purpose; that victory did not give us security, because its outstanding lesson had not been learned, the lesson, namely, that if power is to deter aggression, the aggressor must know beforehand that he will have to meet the power. That truth I have insisted is almost a truism. In the nature of the case power must fail as a deterrent if this element of predictability is absent.

But that is not at all the lesson that was commonly drawn.

That policy could, of course, only take the form of some kind of "Peace Front" as Lord Halifax terms it: as many nations as possible getting together and saying: "If you attack any one of us you attack all." For unless the front had that collective character an aggressor could break it up in detail, isolating first one member and destroying him, then another and so on.[2] Where a number of lesser states confront a great one they must hang together or hang separately; their de-

[2] We feel that if nations were to live always under no law but the law of might, their life would exist only under constant threat, and on those terms life becomes intolerable. Accordingly, we have been, and are, working to unite with ourselves those who feel the same—not with any intention hostile to any other nation, but with a single and perfectly clear resolve to throw all we can into the scales on the side of law as opposed to lawlessness in Europe. (21 June 1939. Viscount Halifax, at the Annual Dinner of 1900 Club.)

fence must be collective, or they can have no defence at all.

But no sooner was the war over and its problem began to be boring, than strange confusions and hostilities revealed themselves about the collective method. A favourite argument ran something like this:

The purpose of collective action is peace. But if you have to go to war to defend one of the members you have just plain war, exactly like war by the old alliances. There is no difference.

There was, of course, profound difference in collective action as embodied in the Covenant. The purpose and the effect of the old type of Alliance was to say to those against whom it was directed: "You must submit to our decision in the disputes which have provoked our alliance. We shall be the judge." The League type of alliance says, on the contrary: "Our Peace Front offers you third-party judgment, or means of conciliation or redress by which we ourselves are prepared to abide. It does not ask you to submit to us, but to the rules which we ourselves accept."

This distinction was completely disregarded. It is doubtful even if it was ever understood by the most vocal critics of the collective system.

Thus "Scrutator" (*Sunday Times*, 14 April 1934) argues that it is no use building up a collective *bloc* for peace, because a much solider *bloc* than we could hope to create did not preserve the peace in 1914. Under the heading "Remember 1914," he writes:

> What made the World War was not the quarrel between Austria and Serbia as it then was, nor even the political rivalry between Germany and Russia in the gates of the East, but the system of alliances and counter-alliances which blew up a local quarrel into a world conflagration. . . .
>
> The beginning of wisdom in Europe is to realize that this mischief of alliances and counter-alliances is just as dangerous now as in 1914, and is not in the least mended by calling it collective security or invoking the name of the League of Nations. The letter kills; only in the spirit is there health. It follows that we shall mediate most effectually in proportion as we keep our independence. . . .
>
> Though the doctrine may be unfashionable these days—there is solid political virtue in minding your own business and keeping your own doorstep clean.

And "Scrutator" adds this strange passage:

> And if we had known in 1914 that we should be joined by the United States, Italy, and Japan, and that all the Dominions would rush to our assistance, should we not then have been more confident in this collective security than we have any right to be in a combination between Russia, Italy and France now—with Russia threatened by Japan, Italy ill at ease with Yugoslavia, Poland covering

the German eastern frontier, and the United States not even belatedly in the struggle this time on our side? Yet that system of collective security did not prevent the Great War.

Let us disentangle a few tangles.

The alliances which preceded the war of 1914 did not represent a collective system at all. They lacked nearly all the elements indispensable thereto. The Grand Alliance did not exist as a peace-time combination. The essence of collective defence is that it should represent a combination of power sustaining a rule which will afford some measure of protection to all members, membership being completely open to the potential or putative aggressor. The power of the Allied combination in 1914 did not offer protection.

The armed law within the state does not merely say to the individual citizen: "Break the law and we imprison you." It gains its permanent power from the fact that the law also says: "Observe the law and it will protect you." Any real League, supported by the power of its constituent members, offers in return for support, security. Unless it does this, it does not embody in any proper sense of the term a collective system at all. The old pre-war type of Alliance embodied no such system of mutual defence. The larger grouping of the Allied powers did not, indeed, exist as a peace-time fact. It offered no security to Germany; there was no element of mutual assistance, no promise to her to protect her against aggression (as for instance from Russia) in return for peaceful settlement of disputes. She had nothing to depend upon for the defence of her rights in any dispute except her own power to overcome her rivals, so that our power was a menace to her as hers was a menace to us.

As already noted, we found much of the Left and much of the Right joining hands in attack on the collective system, on the basis of these confusions.

Thus we find an eminent Conservative author quoting with approval a speech made by Mr. James Maxton against the idea of collective security. Maxton argues that you had collective action in 1914:

> There was a great array of the nations to restrain an aggressor in the interests of international law. You had military, economic and financial sanctions, oil sanctions, and a blockade; the Suez Canal was closed to the aggressor; the Straits of Gibraltar were closed to the aggressor. The Straits of Dover were closed to the aggressor. You smashed Germany flat. You won, and here is the aggressor again.[3]

And so, concludes Maxton, armed resistance is futile. And an eminent Conservative protagonist

[3] See *The Faith of an Englishman*. (Macmillan.)

of conscription, of a greater navy, a greater army
and a greater air force, of every form of armed
resistance, says of Mr. Maxton's argument:

> If anyone knows the answer to that argument,
> he ought to produce it. None has yet been pro-
> duced by the Covenanters.

Mr. Maxton was pleading for pacifism, for let-
ting the totalitarians do their damnedest and not
attempting to resist them, and his argument was
therefore sound—as sound as when he supported
Mr. Chamberlain's action at Munich. Maxton
accepts the logical consequences of Munich, but
the whole Tory party says that when the treatment of Czecho-Slovakia is applied to us we must
resist; we must not acquiesce in it. We must arm
and arm and arm and make all the necessary alliances. So be it. We do so and we win. What then
happens to the alliances and the arms? They are
not to remain, as the instrument of law, as the
means by which the weak are to be permanently
defended against violence, for that, says the critic
from the Right just quoted—and here we come to
one of the strange confusions of this discussion—
would be to coerce the stronger and to provoke
war. That is to say, that as soon as defence becomes a common and mutual defence, embodied
in peace-time organization, it becomes "coercive";
as soon as a group of nations stand together for

mutual aid in resistance to the aggression, create a
defensive federalism for permanent security, they
threaten the world with permanent war.

The Conservative critic already quoted, arguing against the general method of collective defence, of standing together for mutual defence of
national territory, the integrity of frontiers as defined in Article X of the Covenant, says:

> Article X has become the cardinal tenet of a new
> fanaticism for which it fills the universe. Nothing,
> we are told, must ever be conceded to force. Force
> must be met with force. However powerful the
> challenge to League principles, it must be over-
> thrown by that same arbitrament to which it had
> appealed—the Sword. Satan must be expelled, even
> though it be through Beelzebub. European civiliza-
> tion is at stake, and that civilization must deny and
> degrade and torture itself in order to survive.[4]

The so-called coercive articles of the Covenant
(X and XVI) are simply defensive. They set up
a Peace Front in resistance to aggression on the
principle that an attack on one is an attack on all.

The Prime Minister himself has since eight
o'clock on Friday evening, 17 March, warmly supported this principle, though a member of his
Cabinet heatedly attacked it on the evening of
Wednesday, 15 March. The clearest enunciation
of the collective principle was made by Mr. Cham-

[4] *The Faith of an Englishman.* (Macmillan.) p. 164.

berlain in the House of Commons on 3 April, in these terms:

> Whatever may be the ideological differences between Britain and Russia, they do not really count in a question of this kind.
>
> What we are concerned with is to preserve our independence. When I say our independence, I do not mean this country alone. I mean the independence of all States which may be threatened by aggression.
>
> We therefore welcome the co-operation of any country whatever may be its internal system of government, in resistance to aggression.

The defensive principle of the Covenant could not be more clearly expressed.

But note the kind of way in which that perfectly clear principle has been for years confused in so much political literature coming from the Right. The author of the book already quoted from, speaking of the mutual guarantees of independence and territorial integrity embodied in Article X, says:

> To argue for the dragooning of nations as though they were rebels against society, is to argue for war and war and war, not for peace. . . . If we are to force obedience to our code upon such societies at the point of the sword, let us realize on what kind of project we shall be embarking. We shall not be rounding up a gang of law-breakers, enemies of

society without moral support. On the contrary, we shall be waging a war of religion against powerful cultures which hold their views of right and wrong as strongly and sincerely as we hold our own. Italy resorted to war in order, she said, to force a higher civilization upon the Abyssinian people. We have been exhorted to resort to war in order to force a higher civilization upon the Italians. In this matter Italy's claim is, in fact, stronger than ours, since she can certainly do more for civilization by conquering Ethiopia than we can do for it by conquering her. And if we deny her right to forward her concept of civilization by force of arms, how can we claim such a right ourselves? (pp. 170-1).

This critic goes even further. There is no moral distinction, he argues, between defence and aggression, since "War is War."

If I am to take up arms to prove that the taking up of arms is a crime against humanity, I am surely no better than my neighbour who takes up arms merely to prove that he can use them better than I can and is therefore entitled to govern me. His object and mine, his method and mine, become precisely similar. I am to rule him by force, or he is by force to rule me. If I denounce Hitler for imposing his creed by force upon the German people and proceed in the name of progress to impose my own creed by force upon him, I am surely denying and destroying that for which I myself stand and

enthroning that for which I condemn my an-
tagonist.

The above was written before the guarantees
to Poland. We have since formed a Peace Front,
and because one of its members was attacked we
are at war.

When would those who have repudiated Peace
Fronts in the past bring that defensive combination to an end? When, war having come, Germany is defeated? Then we shall repeat what happened in 1918. The Grand Alliance, which fought
the war, almost immediately went to pieces. And
that is why we are now, twenty years after the
last victory, in danger of having to fight another
war to get another victory which, presumably,
will not last longer than the former one. It is not
a cheering prospect. Or shall we maintain the alliance with these mutual commitments as between
Britain and France, and Turkey, with others in
the offing? Recreate, that is, the League?

But that is the very thing against which a host
of critics of the "Scrutator" school have argued so
eloquently and elaborately all these years—and
will begin so to argue again if and when the crisis
passes, unless we can clear up these misunderstandings.

The root of much of this strange argumentation
is a hopeless confusion between defence and coer-

cion. If our armies were to be used to prevent Italian forces conquering Kenya or invading Kent, not even the back-bench Tory would dream of calling the thing "coercion." But if we, with others, use arms to prevent Italy invading Abyssinia, it *is* "coercion." Neither is coercion. Germany and Italy have merely to refrain from killing other people and they will have nothing to fear from the "league against aggression" whether the old or the new. When a group of states form themselves into a federation to help each other in resisting attack upon them, they don't "coerce" the attacker unless all defence is coercion.

But the confusion between defence and coercion is complicated by a further confusion, by the assumption that all change must involve war; that to get change we must permit war. Again we may quote a Conservative critic to illustrate the confusion.

> On a literal reading of Article X, co-operation between France, Germany and Britain is impossible—for the plain reason that it must mean everything they desire for France and Britain, but nothing for Germany. Article X is the crux. (p. 164).

And on another page:

> I am profoundly convinced that the forces in Europe which support the League cannot in a military sense, attempt to contain or smother those

which defy the League without making another great European war inevitable (p. 155).

The common assumption is that if a state is guaranteed security it will adamantly refuse to make any concessions on behalf of necessary changes in the *status quo*. But the contrary comes nearer to the truth. Suppose a state has within its borders a national minority and is asked to cede the minority area. To do so weakens the state strategically. It says to Europe: "If as the result of weakening myself, by making this concession, I am attacked, will you, my neighbour, Europe, help defend me?" And if the neighbours, repudiating such commitments as dangerous, say "no" can we reasonably expect the state in question to make the concession? Security is usually the condition *sine qua non* of peaceful change. To weaken the guarantees against war with some muddled idea that by allowing the strong now and again to have their little war of conquest while we look the other way, we may bring about the necessary changes with the least risk to ourselves, is precisely the type of muddle-headedness which has brought us to our present pass.

To allow the strong to enforce territorial redistribution by war, prompted by the idea that redistribution so secured will make for peace, is to disregard all experience and the most elementary logic of the situation.

Not only do changes made at the will of the victor after war inevitably create as many problems as they solve, but they do not solve *the* problem of war, which is security, that self-preservation which is as much the first law of life with political as with other living organisms. Where self-preservation depends upon the preponderant power of the individual (whether state or person), upon being stronger than those who might attack us, there can, obviously, be no such thing as general defence, for the defence of the stronger in that case is purchased at the cost of sacrificing the defence of the weaker. Only when the law—primarily the supreme law that there shall be no war, that none shall be the victim of his neighbour's violence—is upheld by a sufficiently large group of the human community, can defence become generalized, and reconcilable with justice.

§

Not only is it true that if the force is to deter aggression the aggressor must know he will have to meet it; but the potential aggressor must know something else: that the law he observes will assure him protection. If not he will find his own means of protection—in preponderant power, which becomes a danger to others.

The fact that for years these confusions, the net result of which was a drift towards an almost

American isolationism, stood for a large and important element of public opinion, especially public opinion behind the government, had this importance: the foreign governments most concerned, the German, the Russian, and the neutrals, had to satisfy themselves what our permanent policy was likely to be; how, when the time came, we should really interpret our formal obligations. Upon that depended their own policy. Germany was confronted by the question: "How far can a policy of making impossible any European combination against us by destroying in detail its separate elements, be carried?" The question for Russia, was: "Would Britain really come to our aid if Germany decided upon an attack, or shall we as an alternative to alliance with the West, be compelled to make the best bargain we can with Germany?" And in the case of the lesser states of Europe the question was: "Do Britain and France stand for the law against aggression as a principle, or only when their direct interests seem threatened? If action by Britain and France is doubtful, we are likely to make more probable, rather than less probable, for us the fate of Manchuria, Abyssinia, by joining any Peace Front or collective system." In judging the future policy of a democracy with changing governments public opinion counts for more than formal declaration of Ministers.

Any of the foreign governments above enumerated is likely to judge the value of formal commitments in the light of such statements as those coming from a great English churchman, a moral leader, who is also a man of letters, and commentator, who writes:

It was the naval arrangement with France which above all made it almost impossible for us to stand out in 1914, though we were as little concerned with Serbia then as we are with Czecho-Slovakia now. But we allow ourselves to be entangled without realizing it, and we are then told that honour requires us to keep to our agreements.

Is it true that we are deeply entangled now? Can the French, who have deceived us again and again —about Turkey and Greece, about Italy and Abyssinia, and about neutrality in Spain—drag us into a quarrel with Germany, which might be the end of us as a Great Power, and the end of European civilization?

We are told that we are pledged. I am more inclined to agree with Lord Beaverbrook, who wrote three years ago: "There are no commitments which the British people cannot bring to an end, as soon as they resolve to do so. There are no pledges which cannot be honourably terminated. Are we bound by Locarno? Certainly not."[5]

Even after Munich the newspaper—member of a powerful group—from which the above was

[5] The Very Rev. W. R. Inge, D.D., in the *Evening Standard*, 29 June 1938.

taken, insists that Britain must on no account be committed to continental action:

> The *Evening Standard* has warned the public of this peril. Here it has been pointed out a hundred times that if British policy abroad was to persist in building up commitments to other states, then we should one day be presented with the bill to be paid in full and on the instant.
>
> All our present resources, immense as they are, have hardly availed us to avoid that moment and that settlement now. Our vast financial strength, our powerful industrial equipment, the huge populations and vast, rich territories which we control, have not sufficed to keep us safe from the threat of imminent war.[6]
>
> This Central European cockpit of dissension and war is not an area in which Britain should ever have meddled.[7]

In the midst of the September 1938 crisis, the *Daily Express* announced for the benefit of Germany, in large headlines, "Britain won't Fight." And within a week or two of the outbreak of war the *Sunday Express*[8] tells us:

> We should turn our minds for a time away from Eastern Europe. We should leave off our consideration of the futile and abortive negotiations with Russia. We should abandon the notion of sending

[6] *Evening Standard,* 29 September 1938.
[7] *Evening Standard,* 1 October 1938.
[8] 23 July 1939.

our golden treasure to the Poles and cease to provide payment of the salaries of the officers in the
Polish Army.

The settlement of Polish affairs in relation to
Germany should be left to Colonel Beck, who is a
thoroughly popular and entirely familiar figure in
Berlin.

With Poland out of the way we can give some
thought to our domestic concerns.

There are other elementary confusions which
have bedevilled understanding of policy ever since
the war.

We saw that collective security rested ultimately
upon force, arms. We saw further that great powers were out of the League; that the League was
not the League of the original intention; fulfilment
of our obligation to aid in resistance to aggression;
to defend the victim, and vindicate law, might
involve us in war against great powers. Some
argued: "Let us get out of the League commitments: repudiate that aspect of the League altogether; get rid of Article XVI, Article X."

This "flight from the Covenant" in British opinion assumed during the years 1936, 1937, 1938,
truly tremendous proportions, as some of the Press
comments and letters to the Press here quoted
show. But we did not seem to ask whether our
abandonment of the League or Half League would
in fact reduce the likelihood of our having to use

force for our own defence against very great powers, or whether if we had to resist aggression for our own security it would be better to act on behalf of a formally defined world interest, world law, or merely because we had decided that our own—not universal—security demanded it.

Should we be in any worse position to-day if instead of fighting because Mr. Chamberlain had suddenly in March, completely reversed British foreign policy, and given a guarantee to Poland, we were fighting because we had consistently stood by the League, and were determined to vindicate its rule?

Again and again this writer has insisted that if the collective principle (which an older generation called the Concert of Europe) went to pieces we should sooner or later be faced again with some attempted domination of Europe by a Continental power, which we would resist; that our own domination through sea power which had worked more or less well since Waterloo and had given some sort of order was no longer feasible; and that the road to our own security, to put it on the most "realist" plane was to make our power formally the instrument of a nascent world constitution whatever its defects might be.

A certain critic of the Left, standing in this respect for a considerable group of critics, explains that he approves the League idea in theory, admitting that only by some such institution can the peace of the world be established. He recognized, moreover, that "in order to be in a position to supersede national sovereignties, the authority of such a Government must be backed by force"; that the League might be a chrysalis of such an authority and that pacifists like himself were "up to the time of the Abyssinian fiasco prepared to cherish and succour it." He goes on:

Things being as they are, we find it difficult to regard the League as being anything but a Balance of Power alliance on the old lines dressed up in a new guise; an association of ex-burglars, grown respectable on the enjoyment of past loot, banded together to discourage new recruits to the profession, with a number of respectable, but timid householders hanging on their tails.

We can see difficulties, therefore, in asking a League so conceived to use force against the aggressor and in defence of public right. . . . I even found myself wondering whether the League of Nations—the League, of course, as it now is—should be encouraged to "study the possibility of establishing an international police force to safeguard world peace." For how could such a police force have any title to be considered international, lacking, as it must needs lack, contingents from America, Japan, Germany, or Italy? And how would it not be regarded by Germany and Italy as an army recruited by the democratic Powers, in theory to protect themselves against the Fascist Powers, in practice to menace the Powers against whom it professed to be protection?[9]

Let us see what this means.

The great danger to peace and justice, argues this critic, lies in (a) the old Balance of Power alliance in which (b) successful burglars combine to hold on to their loot; a situation in which (c) force cannot become the instrument of public right or be considered international because it lacks contingents from America, Japan, Germany and Italy, and will therefore (d) be regarded by the Fascist States not as a protection against them but a menace to them.

Such a situation being the great danger to peace, we will, continues the argument, abolish the League, or cease to support it, or put it in cold storage, or deny it power, in any case add from the Left of politics to that flood of disparagement and scepticism which has always assailed it from the Right.

So be it.

Does the fact of abandoning the League, or abolishing it, or putting it in cold storage, or denying it power, get rid of any of those elements of danger above enumerated in (a) (b) (c) or (d)? Does the fact of winding up the League, or abandoning its advocacy, or disparaging it, or creating

[9] *Time and Tide.*

hopelessness and scepticism as to the feasibility of
its principles, get rid of force in international affairs? Or the old type of rival alliance? Or the
combination of Haves against Have-nots? Or
lessen the determination of the successful burglars
to hold on to their loot or cause Germany, Italy
and Japan to regard the Anglo-French-Russian
combination as less threatening to them? Or lessen
the potential virulence of the force which the nations pile up more feverishly than ever?

I suggest that:

(1) Every one of the dangers cited as reason
for refusing support of the League at the present
time will be increased by the withdrawal of that
support.

(2) By refusing to associate our force with a
League policy we do not diminish the sum total
of force in the world, we increase it; we do not
take a step towards its elimination from international affairs, but towards making it more dangerous, more ruthless, more anarchic. By refusing
commitment of our power to the defence of public
right as the political mechanism by which we
secure our national defence, and by reserving it
solely as the instrument of purely national interests as we conceive them, we do something more
than take force out of law, we take all law out of
force; we take a restraining hand from our own
use of force, give greater freedom to those who

would use it as an instrument of national or imperial policy; greater freedom for its use to maintain exclusions and inequalities that threaten peace.

(3) The only means by which military alliances (like that which we maintain with France) can be prevented from becoming what they have always been in the past—the prelude to war—is to make them the instrument of a League policy, by making them subject, that is, to the submission of disputes to third-party judgment; the full discussion of grievance; the maintenance of organs of peaceful change; the development of equality of economic opportunity for nations.

(4) The reasons for guiding our own foreign policy by League principles, League policy, are not weakened by the fact of the secession of the United States, Germany, Italy, and Japan.

(5) If the argument that force for League purposes once granted would be used by reactionaries for reactionary purposes, had any validity; if, that is, the reactionaries hoped to find in the League a convenient instrument of reactionary ends, they would be supporters of the League. They are not. Very much the contrary is the case. The groups most reactionary in economic and social policy— the Beaverbrooks, Rothermeres, Amerys, Page-Crofts, Lord Lloyds—are precisely those who are most implacable in their hatred of and hostility

to any effective League, and who for the most
part bluntly demand its abolition (as did Lord
Stonehaven in the House of Lords recently).

Let us particularize.

We have a virtual alliance with France by
which we are committed to her defence, and
should be so committed even if the attack upon
her were the result, not of any quarrel, properly
speaking, of her enemy with us or even with her,
but with one of her allies, say, Russia. The danger
to Britain from the destruction of French independence would be just as great whether it re-
sulted largely from France's own fault, the provocative character of her policy, or whether she
were the victim of pure aggression. We were the
allies of Russia in 1914 (as earlier of Turkey) not
because Russia was right and Germany wrong,
but because considerations of our own security
pushed us to that alliance.

The present alliance with France will not be
abandoned, nor shall we "disinterest" ourselves
in her security. It is part of our defensive power
which we shall not surrender even if our allies
behave very badly indeed with their neighbours.

That being the case, the best chance of seeing
that the policy of our allies does not lead them,
and so us, into war, is to get them to accept sound
principles of international behaviour, such as
those embodied in the League: full hearing of

grievances, third-party judgment, equality of right, means of peaceful change, principles acceptable to those whose aggressions we fear.

In certain cases, acceptance of such a policy by potential allies will mean a sacrifice of strength. That sacrifice they will not make unless we agree to support them if they are attacked as the result of making it. But we should have to support them in any case. To make the League policy the condition of our alliance does not add to our liabilities and does diminish the risk.

One notes the progression in confusion.

Thus we find Lord Astor protesting:

> To-day the people of Britain are seriously asking themselves whether the present political, geographic, and economic *status quo* is so fair as to justify them in committing themselves to fight to preserve it unless and until nations including ourselves can voluntarily agree to its amendment and are prepared to make some contribution thereto.
>
> Plunging into war to defend every detail of the *status quo* would split the country and shatter the Empire whether this war is called "collective security" or "mutual assistance."
>
> Unfortunately the Covenant and present League cannot effect such political, geographic, or economic changes as impartial third party judgment would consider necessary. Until effective machinery has brought about peaceful revision, the Covenant pledge is merely an unlimited undertak-

ing to go to war to maintain in its entirety a *status quo* which few now consider just or the basis of lasting peace.

We were under no obligation, of course, to resist change of the *status quo*. We are under obligations to resist its change by war. We got rid of the obligations (virtually) but that did not rid us of the liability—for we found ourselves in a year or two at war in resistance to an attempt to change the *status quo* by war, a change by free negotiation would not have brought us to war.

Already a year before, Lord Lothian had been urging the elimination of the Sanctions Clauses from the League:

The Abyssinian case proves that, while the League Powers were willing to put economic pressure on an aggressor, they have not been prepared to face the only method by which they could have vindicated their authority—the police war, which seemed likely to follow oil sanctions or the severance of Italian communications with East Africa. Common sense revolts from the logic which says that we should risk the killing of millions of innocent non-combatants all over Europe (with no lasting peace at the end of it) which must be the risk if a League which no longer contains a majority of the Great Powers attempts to coerce a Great Power to the point of war. . . .

The only honourable course is that we should

give notice, at once, that we must eliminate from the Covenant an obligation to go to war all over the world which neither we nor the Dominions are willing, or in fact are able, to live up to. Neither we nor Europe can formulate a policy which will be stable, because nations know the points at which the nations are prepared to go to war, until this uncertainty is removed. Moreover, only then shall we be able to preserve or revive the League as a universal instrument for international conciliation and co-operation and, where sufficient agreement can be reached, for joint pressure (which is all it can be so long as we retain national sovereignty) and not as the international war office it must remain so long as the Covenant contains an automatic obligation which can only be discharged by going to war.

The next thing is to settle down to organize security on a regional basis, because we now see that M. Litvinov's famous phrase "peace is indivisible" in reverse means "all wars shall be world wars."[10]

Which, of course, involves the fallacies we have already discussed. If, as already noted, Abyssinia had been a British colony (so that Britain's defence of it had been certain), there would have been no war: Italy would not have attacked, no question of killing millions of non-combatants all over Europe.

[10] *Times,* 5 May 1936.

Furthermore, if in truth, the aggressor really foresaw that all wars were to be world wars, he would not risk aggression. When the whole world is prepared to concern itself with the prevention of any war, war will end.

For years we have been attempting such locali-zation of war—which is precisely what Germany has been attempting. She too would localize all her wars; eliminate from her dispute with Czecho-Slovakia any interference of the outside world. This localization is Hitler's constant demand. The fate of Poland is nobody's concern but his and Russia's. For some years our policy was precisely this localization.

How far, by the way, those of this particular school of political thought, were prepared to carry this regional policy is revealed in the writing of another member of the school, Mr. J. L. Garvin. During 1937 Mr. Garvin was prepared to recom-mend that Poland, Austria, Czecho-Slovakia, Yugoslavia, Roumania, Hungary and Bulgaria be brought under German domination, constituting a German Federation. He recommended it on the ground that "the German race should have a scope comparable to that of the Soviet Empire." Of such a German Empire, he wrote:

It would comprehend most of that great geo-graphical sphere in farther Europe, dislocated and disorganized by the war-treaties in the name of emancipation—"Balkanized" as the vivid and true phrase went amongst all intelligent pacifists. The second of the main conditions of constructive peace in Europe as a whole is that a large part of "Eastern Europe" proper shall be reconstructed under German leadership.

The eastward sphere concerned lies between the Germanic centre of the Continent and the Soviet boundaries. The most vital part of it stretches down the Danube. Not for nothing in the politics of to-day as in past history does the Danube, that longest river-artery of Europe, draw its head-waters from the Reich before it flows far onward through or by many nations to the Black Sea. Through or by Germanic Austria, mixed Czecho-Slovakia, dismembered Hungary, redoubtable though ill-united Yugoslavia, penalized Bulgaria, and New Roumania. These far-stretching territories, naturally connected, but now split up beyond all reason by racial antagonisms and the consequent restrictive economics, are the seismic region or "earthquake zone" of European affairs. Their present conditions contain more acute causes of future war apt to spread into general war than all the rest of the Continent put together.

So he would unite them economically by a customs union, though, unlike the old German Zollverein, not on the basis of full trade within the

Federation, but something it would seem along the lines of a Central European Ottawa. Thus:

The precedent is furnished by the great network of preferential treaties which, in the twenty years before the War, were negotiated by Germany throughout all the areas we have mentioned, and to the remarkable advantage of all concerned.

He adds:

For illumination on the nature of the present case, though not on its extent, let us all remember the profound prophecy not of a German but of one of the founders of the modern Czech revival, Francis Pallatzky. "If Austria did not exist it would have to be invented." And this holds true in the spirit though the reconstruction necessary would now have to be carried out on a magnificent scale, as we have seen. The historic Hapsburg monarchy, though an obsolete political structure in its last period, was an admirable economic system, with far better conditions of general human welfare and progress than now exist where it stood among the disrupted fragments and the "Balkanized" discords of the separated states. They ought to be as efficiently connected with each other and with Germany along the whole course of the Danube as are the American states along that other "ole man river," the Mississippi.

In other words, the whole plan is pretty much

what we accused Germany of desiring to do before the last war, and which we entered that war to prevent. She would probably have achieved just such a purpose as that described by Mr. Garvin if we and our Allies had not made war upon her.

CHAPTER XI

THE RUSSIAN EPISODE
AND THE FUTURE

The fact which emerges so far from the Russian episode is that for Russia considerations of political security, the assurance of being free from outside attack, override "ideological" considerations. It is a fact which should make possible co-operation with her for the purely political purpose of common security.

IN ALL the strange convolutions of Russian policy, one fact stands out. Russia, like merely "Capitalist" states, seeks first of all defence, the means of living secure from outside interference the kind of life she has chosen. In the associates which she chooses in the international field she places that need of security far above preferences based on doctrinal or ideological considerations. The promotion of Communism may be one objective. The political security of the Russian state is another, and if the two came into conflict, then the first must, it would seem quite clear, give way to the second.

We have been desirous of avoiding an "ideological war" based on the conflict of Communism with Capitalism or a *bourgeois* order of society.

If we had pursued the purpose of common security with the energy we might have done, the effect would have been to encourage Russia to co-operate with us in achieving that end of security by collective means. As it is she has turned to other means.

Let us look at certain outstanding facts.

It was clear in the first few days of the war that Polish resistance would rapidly collapse; that Britain and France could do nothing to stem the collapse, and that unless Russia intervened the whole country would be under the control and in the occupation of Germany. That result would constitute an intolerable menace to the security of Russia, in a direct and immediate as well as in a more remote sense. For the whole of Versailles Poland to come under German occupation would add enormously to the war resources of Germany, would lead inevitably to the conquest of the Ukraine and put Germany in a position to carry out the *Mein Kampf* programme at Russia's expense.

What in that situation, as it existed at the beginning of September, was the chief of a state in Stalin's position to do? What would any statesman in the world, Socialist or Capitalist, having regard to the security of his nation, have done? Stood by and watched the rapid undermining of his country's defensive position until he found himself at the mercy of an enemy who had on numberless occasions expressed the intention of destroying the Russian Government and regime? Help defend Poland? But Poland, by refusing in the preceding negotiations to permit Russian troops to enter Polish territory, refused in fact Russian aid in the only form in which it would be effective. Again, there is no statesman in the world who would have accepted such a condition. In other words, if Stalin had been actuated by one single motive, the defence of Russia in the least costly way in which the conditions of European politics of the year 1939 permitted, he would have acted exactly as he has done. In so doing he has placed the immediate political and military security of Russia and her freedom from war above the permanent security of Europe as a whole; he has been unmindful of the safety of others; has contributed his part to an appalling world anarchy, chaos, lawlessness and disorder. So be it. But is there a single nation in Europe or America this last few years that has placed the general, long-term security of others before its own immediate safety? Britain? France? One recalls the familiar list of Manchuria, China, Abyssinia, Austria, Spain, Albania, Czecho-Slovakia. The United States? The lesser States of Europe? Do we regard their complete neutrality ("When others are attacked and destroyed, we are unconcerned, neutral; nothing to do with us"), their quite un-abashed avowal that so long as they are secure the rest of the world may perish, as very shame-ful? For years, until a few weeks since, we—British statesmen, editors, writers, commentators—de-clared this isolationist morality to be natural, in-evitable, right and that for a nation to sacrifice itself for some general principle of law or right as embodied in the defence of strange distant coun-tries—Manchuria, Abyssinia, China, Czecho-Slo-vakia—was a course which only fanatical war-mongering Genevafists would counsel.

Russia could not in the circumstances as they existed in September 1939, have taken any course better calculated than the one she did take to protect, as cheaply as possible and with as little suffering as possible to the Russian people, the defensive position of the Russian nation. That would have been as true if Russia had been a Capi-talist state as it is true when she happens to be a Communist one.

Which indicates that outstanding fact of the situation to which reference was made at the be-ginning of this chapter. Russia did not come to the bargain with the anti-Communist Hitler be-cause she was a Communist state, but because she felt herself to be a threatened state, endangered by the growing power of Germany. Russia has turned to the game of power politics, has adopted "imperialistic" methods not because she seeks markets or "profits," but because she seeks, and is in a world of anarchy compelled to seek, as the sole condition of survival, the maintenance of her proportionate power in the world, her strategic military position. If that goes, her defence would go, for she would be at the mercy of others. And that is as true, we now see, of a Socialist state as of a Capitalist one. If Russia had happened now to be a Capitalist state, her action in conquering a large part of Poland would have been attributed by Communists, Socialists, Radicals, Progressives, the Left as a whole the world over, as due to the desire of Russian capitalists for markets, the push of the profit motive. The event is sufficient commentary on that explanation.

Because our success in the war depends so largely upon understanding the forces which have provoked it, the motives which underlie the policies of the combatants, this matter is a good deal more than one of abstract doctrine. It is very near to the urgencies of the moment.

The Prime Minister's statement that our war aim is to "enable the peoples of Europe to preserve their independence and their liberties" has been so often repeated that it has now become our battle cry. Very good. That purpose has always been the problem of peace in Europe—to secure the defence of each in such a way that the security of the stronger did not kill the security of the weaker. It was the aim of the last war (Mr. Chamberlain's statement is simply a paraphrase of several made by Mr. Asquith in 1914) and we failed to achieve that aim. How are we now to succeed?

It has been a long-held theory among Progressives that the major effort and the first effort in the accomplishment of this end should be directed at an economic change, because, ran the doctrine, the ultimate cause of war lay in the need of capitalism for profits, markets, and because this is inherent in the capitalist system and operates even when individual capitalists may sincerely detest war. The roots, it is insisted, are economic.

This writer (to the dismay it would seem of so many of his friends on the Left) has always challenged that view and held that the forces which make for war are much more political than economic, are to be found in the need of states for power to the point of predominance as the sole instrument of defence—that is to say self-preservation, survival—in a sphere where no commonly supported law or constitution exists; that this drive to the acquisition of power is much more potent and dangerous than purely economic forces are apt to be, for the psychological reason that men love power and domination much more than they love welfare and comfort; and more destructive for the mechanical reason that, given the international anarchy, national power must in the end defeat itself as a means of defence because it must always be competitive and relative: A's security depends upon being stronger than B, which kills B's security; a fact which will prompt B to return the compliment.

The struggle for power, for domination, is thus far more competitive than the struggle for markets. The purpose of the capitalist in his search for wealth is not defeated by an increase in the wealth of other nations; his purpose is almost always promoted thereby. But the purpose of the statesman looking first and foremost to the security of his nation *is* defeated by the growing power of another—as Stalin has testified by his course of policy this last few months. He has afforded us the spectacle of a Socialist state pushed like Capitalist states to the pursuit of power as the sole means of defence. He has, in fact, always recognized this truth that a Socialist state is confronted by precisely the same political difficulties of security as a Capitalist state; that indeed the success of his own Socialist purpose might well depend on such political relations with Capitalist states as would ensure common security. Russia has been ready in the past to undertake to fight for Capitalist states (witness the Franco-Soviet Alliance—apart from the League obligations) if Capitalist states were prepared to fight for her. The political purpose of security could be common to Capitalist and Socialist states alike.

The Russian occupation of Poland is due not primarily to the fact that Russia has turned "imperialist" in a sense in which she was not before, that she is seeking markets, "profits for her capitalists." It is due to the fact that the West having rejected the collective security in which she was prepared to co-operate she has had to turn to the development of her own national power as the only available alternative, however precarious that may be.

But note what it is likely to involve. Russia was determined that, rather than face the complete German domination of Eastern Europe she would seize positions making her dominant in territories where Germany hoped to be. Already the old contradictions of the method are revealing themselves: if Russia is to be really secure against Germany, then Germany will not be secure against Russia.

Certain facts stand out. Hitler would dearly like to see the Allies come into military conflict with Russia: and there are some in France and Britain quite ready to oblige him. Already, as these lines are being written, the air is full of rumours (referred to previously) of support by the Allies of a revolution from the Right in Germany, possibly monarchist in character, on the understanding that such a German government would join with the Allies, Italy and Japan in an anti-Russian bloc. Hitler could of course frustrate that plot long before it had matured by himself joining up with Stalin. That kind of manœuvre is as silly as it is dangerous.

So far both Germany and Russia have proceeded on the principle of dividing the spoils (i.e. sources of power) instead of fighting about them. And the method obviously can be carried very far. If Japan is introduced into the arrangement it can be carried across the world to the confines of China.

It is unlikely to stop at the mere partition of Poland. The difference already revealed between the invaders concerning "spheres of influence" in Europe—as to how the various lesser states, Baltic, Balkan, or Danubian, shall be distributed as between the two "orbits"—is more likely to end in agreement for division of the spoils than in conflict. We are not in a good position to prevent that division of spoils. It is impossible at present for France and Britain to protect even the democratic lesser states (Norway, Sweden, Finland, Denmark, Holland, Belgium, Switzerland), if only because they refuse to be protected in the sense that they fear to form a defensive combination with us based on mutual assistance.

A dozen lesser states making an effective unit might constitute a force of great defensive power. But if, for any reason, when one is attacked the other eleven remain passive, and then when one of the remaining eleven is attacked the other ten remain passive, it becomes quite evident that the totalitarian combination can destroy the whole group in detail. The rejection of the collective principle of defence has produced that situation.

It reaches beyond Europe. Russia may well come to a bargain with Japan on the basis of the partition of China in some form, as Russia came to a bargain with Germany on the basis of the partition of Poland. Germany, Russia and Japan will thus dominate a geographical area stretching from the Rhine, across Europe, across Asia, to the Pacific, the material resources of which (as well as much of its man-power) will be available for the combination. That combination is likely to hold together so long as there are spoils to share, spoils from victims incapable of effective defence. The maxim that there is nothing two parties will agree about so readily as the spoliation of a third, applies with force in the present situation.

But that kind of partnership has immense dangers for both of the two parties. To place under Russian government—or the prospect of Russian "protection"—passionately anti-Communist elements would be as dangerous for Russia as it would be for Germany to absorb any more anti-Nazi elements, Czechs, Austrians, Slovaks, Jews, Liberals, Social-Democrats.

Stalin probably more than Hitler is conscious of the danger of alien elements within a dictatorship state. It is perhaps one of the reasons why Russia favoured some form of collective security as the instrument of her defence rather than the indefinite territorial expansion which is likely to be the only alternative. There is no reason to suppose that, except for the German menace, Russia would have attempted to regain the territories once hers. Her motive throughout has been her own security.

Can our diplomacy build on this fact?

It is the fashion now (and on the whole a good fashion) to include European federalism among the possibilities of future settlement. But federalism, like socialism, is something that may take numberless forms: the federalism of the British Commonwealth—a federalism limited to defence, and even then only by a "gentleman's understanding"—differs profoundly from the federalism of the United States, as the Cantonal federation of Switzerland differs from both. Any European federalism would have to leave wide divergencies of political, economic and social doctrine to its units, just as there are wide divergencies as between, say, New Zealand and Hyderabad or Jersey and Jamaica in the British system.

We stand for the restoration of Czecho-Slovakia and Poland. But that does not necessarily mean the re-incorporation of, say, Sudeten areas within the new Czecho-Slovakia nor the territories seized by Poland in defiance of the League—and of British protests—in the new Poland. If we accept the principle of federalism—which is that no one, big or little, is entitled to be independent in the literal sense of the term, that everyone accepts some limitation of sovereignty and independence —then there might even now be the possibility of arrangement with both Russia and Italy (the latter of whom might be asked to restore the Negus in Abyssinia to a position like that occupied by the Bey of Tunis in the French Empire). We fulfil the obligations which brought us into the war far more honestly and completely by securing for the victims of aggression—potential or actual —a limited independence which is real and lasting than by the assertion of unqualified "independence" of the old order.

It brings us to the questions which, even if unexpressed, are present in the mind of the public and must be answered if as the war goes on the effort is to be adequately sustained. How, when victory is ours, is the restoration of Poland or Czecho-Slovakia or Austria to be made any more permanent, any longer lived, than the settlement of 1919 has proved to be? The defeat of Germany in 1918, the constitution of Czecho-Slovakia, and the restoration of Poland have lasted twenty years. How long is the next German defeat and the next Polish or Czecho-Slovak restoration to last? Are Britain and France to be called upon every decade or every other decade to "restore" democracies like Poland or Czecho-Slovakia? How is our purpose, even after victory, to be given permanence? Without some feeling that the thing is possible, without at least a design of the new world before us, how can our people be expected to give all that they have and are?

These are tragic questions. It is better to have an answer for them than merely to ignore them. Unanswered they will fester and at vital moments mean indecision, and may well endanger our purpose.

Let us summarize.

If we are ever to restore a Poland of any kind, then sooner or later we shall have to talk not merely or mainly with Germany, but mainly with Russia. Peace talk, whether before or after the defeat of Germany, must mean talking with Russia. It will be more a Russian than a German problem we shall have to settle. For to the degree to which Germany is weakened by our pressure in the field, the relative power of Russia grows. The more that Germany has to concentrate her power on the West to meet ours, she has to withdraw it from the East and increase Russia's. If the defeat of Germany comes about by internal revolution, Russia will probably have more to say to its direction than we shall. She knows more about revolution; her contacts with Germany are closer than ours. If Russia keeps out of the war—as now seems increasingly likely—her potential power grows as that of the belligerents declines.

So we had better decide that if there is to be conference, it should be mainly conference with Russia. The past hesitations of our Conservatives in bringing about the maximum co-operation with Russia have been due presumably to their fear of Bolshevism. The result of their hesitant policy has been enormously to increase the power of Bolshevist Russia and the area of its influence. Are the same fears, prompting the same policy, to be pursued indefinitely with the same results of increasing Bolshevist power? Stupidity, as the Frenchman said, is a great gift, but it should not be abused.

Soviet Russia, it is said, is a dictatorship. So was Tsarist Russia. It did not prevent Republican France and Democratic England seeking alliance with her. Soviet Russia has treated Poland badly. So did Tsarist Russia. It did not prevent our promising Tsarist Russia at the beginning of the last

war that she should have a free hand in the settlement of Poland's destiny.

One fact upon which we could build in the
framing of our policy stands out in the recent behaviour of Russia. She seeks, first and last, beyond
all ideological aims relating to Communism or the
Class War, the preservation of Russia as a state, as
a political entity, safe from outside domination or
interference. She has sought, that is to say, what
we in the West call national security and she has
employed in pursuing that end exactly the same
means which the great capitalist powers have employed in the amoral world of international anarchy.

When it was clear that Poland would collapse,
what state, Socialist as much as Capitalist, would
not have done what Russia did? Poland, having
refused in the preceding negotiations to permit
Russian troops to enter Polish territory, had in fact
made Russo-Polish military co-operation completely impossible. There is no statesman in the
world, putting first the security of his country, but
would, or could have done in that situation other
than what Stalin did. Stalin played power politics
with all the trimmings, because only by so doing
could he keep Russia in a position effectively to
defend herself against an ever-growing Germany.

But for years previously Russia had been trying
genuinely to base her national security upon the

establishment of general collective security. Threatened on two fronts—on the east by Japan, the west by Germany—a system of real collective security in which "peace is indivisible" would obviously have suited her interest best. But she found in those years since she joined the League, both in Conservative France and Conservative Britain, a deep and contemptible scepticism concerning the feasibility of the League system, and, in addition, deep hostility to herself. Is it surprising, therefore, that she gave it up and turned to the older method?

But Stalin's move has proved one thing. Namely, that Russia will put the political purpose of her own security above doctrinal or ideological sympathies. Obviously, there could have been no bargain with Germany save on the basis: "I will leave your internal system alone, if you will leave mine." Only so could the thing have come about at all. That principle of non-interference in the internal affairs of other states, while seeking means of common security, could, after all, be applied more easily to distant pluto-democracies like Britain and France than to a next door Nazi neighbour. We can build on the fact that Russia's interest in security overrides ideologies and internal differences more easily and more safely than can Hitler. If we would.

One word more.

Some of us have always feared that Bolshevist and Nazi "ideologies" were very akin, and their likeness has been the theme of much writing. Undoubtedly the similarity has been on the increase. Mr. Alexander Werth (among others) has pointed out that there was a new spirit coming to the surface in Russia, together with the new men who were replacing the victims of the "purges." "I do not merely mean a nationalist and almost Chauvinist spirit which found expression in the history text-book of Russian schools," he says, "but a spirit curiously akin to Nazism. Already some six or seven years ago there was a Soviet diplomatist, a Mr. Dimitrievsky, who rebelled and fled from the Stockholm Embassy. But, though a rebel, he proclaimed himself a forerunner of the 'new spirit' of which, he already then claimed, Stalin would become the hero and the embodiment. It was a nationalist spirit and imperialist and anti-Semitic."

He goes on to relate how a young Russian "proletarian" novelist who was a delegate to an international writers' congress in Paris in 1935, gave his impressions of the various countries he had visited. Poland was a "miserable, backward country"; France "very pretty and all that, but it's a lot of window-dressing, a façade covering up a lot of rottenness." And then, with genuine admiration, he said, "Ah, but you should see Germany. Now, that's a country where things are well done. And

Hitler is a clever man—just look how he's handled the unemployment problem." He seemed unimpressed by any anti-Fascist arguments, and would say, "Yes, but still they do things well, better even than we do." And more recently a well-known ex-Soviet diplomatist in Paris tried hard to convince me that "we were all 'kidding' ourselves if we believed we should have an alliance with Stalin."

Mr. Werth concludes:

> But "wishful thinking" stopped one from taking such prophecies too seriously. Granted that there were two conflicting policies in Russia, it was our duty to do our best to secure the Russian alliance—if only on paper—to impress Hitler. What gave one confidence, in spite of everything, was the conviction that in the long run, at any rate, Germany's and Russia's interests would clash, just as the interests of Napoleon and the Tsar of Russia clashed, in spite of Tilsit. Tilsit was in 1809; three years later the two monarchs were at war. But it is unfortunate that the new Tilsit should have occurred at this moment, if it was a Tilsit and not something deeper.[1]

Let us assume that this similarity of outlook in the Bolshevist and Nazi outlook is the case. But long before the arrival either of Bolshevism in Russia, or Nazism in Germany, the two countries found association difficult. They went to war when

[1] *Manchester Guardian,* 5 September 1939.

both were imperial regimes. When the Nazi regime is shaken and Germany faced by chaos she will probably be ready enough to accept any form of association which will give her security from Russia. And the Russian rulers are not so secure in their seats that they would want revolution to spread once more to their territory or the influence of German army chiefs—anti-Nazi and anti-Bolshevist alike—to extend to the Russian army. In the final analysis peace and security for both countries will prove the common interest, and should appeal to that common interest of the two states fail, then indeed does unification of the West become imperative.

CHAPTER XII

GRIEVANCES, REVISION AND PEACE

We have the proof of experience that revision of Versailles, even to the extent of restoring to Germany everything she possessed in 1914, would not give peace: when she had it, peace was not kept. The supreme grievance of every state is absence of security. Until that is redressed, the redress of none other counts.

It is a common assumption that the peace failed because Germany suffered under grievances which she was determined to redress by war, and that our next peace will succeed if we treat her justly and give her no ground for grievance.

Such a view indicates a failure to understand the nature of our problem, for it assumes that wars arise because nations have specific grievances, such as those we had with France at the end of the nineteenth century, about Madagascar, Fashoda, Newfoundland, etc.

On the eve of the Great War, the late Sir Edward Grey, as he then was, said: "I can settle with France because we have differences which we can discuss and adjust. I cannot settle with Germany because we have no differences with her at all."

A dozen historians have noted that never were the relations between Germany and England so free from differences as on the eve of the war, differences in the sense that Germany was making upon us certain demands in the way of colonies, or what not, that we were refusing to grant; or that we were making similar demands that she was refusing to grant.

So with this war. It has not arisen because Germany was making upon *us* certain demands in the way of colonies, or what not, that we were refusing. Such things were not the subject of the discussions which ended in war at all. Germany was indeed, it is quite true, offering us peace without asking a single thing of us in the way of a surrender of an inch of territory, or of any national right we then possessed. The quarrel was entirely about a third party, and Germany's behaviour towards that third party, just as the quarrel of 1914 had been about third parties, beginning with Serbia, and going on to Belgium and France.

Yet for twenty years a great many of us have been saying: "Let the parties who are quarrelling settle their differences by direct negotiation, and let us keep out." The advice ignored the most patent realities of the world in which we live, and indicates a complete ignorance of what it is all about, the nature of our problem.

The war of 1914 began in a quarrel between

Austria and Serbia, a quarrel which almost instantly produced an invasion of Belgium. Why should Belgium be invaded by Germany because Austria had made extravagant demands on a Balkan state? And what settlement of grievance as between Germany and Britain would prevent the recurrence of a situation in which the murder of an Archduke in the Balkans would cause the farmers of Dakota to leave their farms, Japanese pearl fishers their fishing, Australians their sheep-runs, Canadian traders their snows and woods, in order to fight Germany in Flanders?

Germany offered Britain peace in 1914, as she offers Britain peace now, as she offers France peace insistently, repeatedly, constantly, saying: "We have no quarrel with you. Why do you want to fight us?"

We and France fought in 1914 because though we failed fully to see the truth and draw the right conclusions in policy, it was a fact that what happened to a rather corrupt little state in the Balkans did concern the whole world, as the whole world was to learn in the misery and tears of untold millions of its people. What Germany does to Czecho-Slovakia and to Poland does concern us, as we have since learned—have had to learn because we failed to draw the lesson from previous experience. We have been compelled once more to fight for a principle of conduct, a law, which we must uphold, on pain of deadly consequences to ourselves if that abstract law should fail of vindication.

It is clear, therefore, that grievances of the specific kind usually implied in the term, are secondary. We had no grievances against Germany in 1914, in this sense, except this supreme grievance: her victory would deprive us of defence, security. Germany has one supreme grievance to-day. If her neighbours are in a position to combine against her, dominate her, she feels she runs the risk of another Versailles. She feels, therefore, that she must dominate her neighbours as the only alternative to being dominated once more by them.

When we talk of the redress of grievances, and the revision of Versailles, and the destruction of Hitler or Hitlerism, as the one adequate road to peace, let us ask a few simple questions.

Pre-war Germany was a relatively liberal and highly prosperous nation. She did not live under the grievances of a Versailles Treaty. Nor was her conduct dictated by a Hitler. She was living under a constitution which permitted a large measure of parliamentary government; the existence, as already noted, of a powerful social democratic party, and a Press and public opinion that was relatively free.

She possessed her colonies, and her foreign

trade had for years been growing by leaps and bounds. She traded freely with the British Empire, and in many of the British colonies, particularly in the African colonies, was often able to beat the British merchants on their own ground. She lived in a relatively Free-Trade world, a world at least of stable currencies, with a universal money in the shape of gold. Her ships sailed freely the seven seas.

Now, suppose that we could undertake a revision so complete that we could put it all back, restore to Germany not merely all her colonies, but all the territory which she possessed in Europe in 1914. That would be "some" revision. But we know by complete proof, the proof of the event, that that of itself would not preserve peace, for when she had all that territory, all those advantages, all those securities, peace was not kept. It is quite clear, therefore, that revision in this sense, restoration, restitution, would not get to the root of the matter.

It may be argued, this assumes that the fault of 1914 lay with Germany. Let us assume then that the fault lay with Britain. And then the point which it is the purpose now to make becomes more clear than ever, for it would prove that however sated an empire may be, whatever territorial advantages she possesses, however democratic her institutions, that will not suffice to preserve peace. To say that the cause of the war lay with Britain, it is to say that the possession of ample living space and the absence of grievances does not prevent war.

And if the Socialist would add that the scramble for territorial expansion is due to the capitalist system, then the evidence of the last few months should throw light on that too. For we have seen a Communist state of vast possessions and resources also proceed to annexation and domination, to the seizure of neighbouring territory, the domination of small states, as ruthlessly as any Capitalist state could have done. And it so proceeded for the same reason that Capitalist states have followed that line of conduct. In the world of anarchy, where there is no law, a state, whether it be Communist, or Capitalist, must for the purpose of self-preservation, survival, enter upon the road of power competition, of conquest.

The purpose common to all states is the purpose of self-preservation, defence, security. If nations are to remain as entities at all, as individuals, their security can only be achieved by the maintenance of a system of mutual aid in defence, the maintenance of a political constitution between them. In this sense it is true to say that the fundamental problem is a political one, not economic. Russia is co-operating with Germany for a political purpose which stands over and above doctrinal differences concerning Socialism, above ideologies.

But if it be true to say that the political purpose comes first, it is also true to say that that political purpose may be rendered impossible by the power of certain economic ideas which it is now worth while to examine.

CHAPTER XIII

AN ASSASSIN THEORY

No law is possible if those asked to support it believe that keeping it would condemn them to poverty or extinction. So long as men believe that national welfare depends on territorial expansion, "living space," and that conquest is just part of man's "struggle for bread," nothing in the way of an orderly society is possible. Those illusions must be unveiled if men are to co-operate for peace.

BRITAIN has been pushed considerably against her will into the defence by war of a principle of international life, the principle that aggression upon any one member of the international community threatens all. She has discovered the supreme need, even from the point of view of her own security, to be to defend the general law, the law of "no aggression, no war."

But certain commonly-accepted assumptions, assumptions indeed all but universally regarded as self-evidently true, have heretofore stood obstinately in the way of the establishment or maintenance of rule or law in the international field.

Any rule or law against violence in international life is impossible, it is argued—and felt often when it is not argued—because it runs counter to a still more imperative law, the law of survival, the struggle for bread, for life.

The theory is quite simple and plausible, granted certain assumptions. According to it, the earth and its resources are strictly limited. Population is not; it is capable of indefinite expansion. Whether, therefore, we, our children, and those to whom we have the most direct responsibility, or others, aliens, foreigners, are to enjoy the fruits of the earth, depends upon our power relatively to theirs, to fight for and to hold our share. You cannot, goes on the argument, settle struggles between nations by elaborate treaties, paper rules, because life itself is involved; you cannot ask whole nations to commit suicide on behalf of universal right.

It is as though (the present writer has used the illustration before) one cannibal were to say to another: "It is clear that either I must eat you, or you must eat me. Let us come to a friendly agreement about it."

They will not come to a friendly agreement about it. They will fight, so long as both believe that the only source of sustenance is the body of the other. And perhaps the point of the story is that they will fight even if it is quite untrue that the only source of food is the body of the other, even though in the tree above their heads there may be ample food unattainable by either acting alone, but perfectly within their reach if one would stand on the shoulders of the other, and the two would then divide the spoils. But that fact would in no way stop their fight until they saw it as a fact; until then they would continue mutual murder, not because there was need for it, but because they wrongly believed there was that need.

The basis of conduct is to be found not in the facts, or in self-interest. It is to be found in what men believe to be the facts, believe to be self-interest. Not the facts, but men's opinions about them are what matter most.

Thirty years ago this writer insisted that we should get no law or constitutional principle in the international field enabling us to establish a system of security, so long as such ideas, vague, muddled, unexamined, but nevertheless powerful, either dominated the minds of men, or lay in wait in the back of their minds, ready to spring upon and destroy any law which seemed to limit their freedom to prey upon others if and when they have the chance. It was no good, he suggested, talking about law if men believe that obedience to law means death.

It was not so much a question of economics, as of biology; not a question whether war paid dividends but whether it furnished the means of life otherwise unattainable. To be forced to forgo the means of life is, men feel, the supreme injustice.

Because it is the feeling of the ordinary busy citizen which determines conduct and policy in this matter, the question, whether it is broadly true or broadly false that a nation's welfare and prosperity depends upon the extent of its territory, its possessions, is one of those questions which must be answered plainly, yes or no. For the busy citizen, the average voter, usually ill-educated, wrapped up in his own affairs, cannot split hairs too finely. Such forces as nationalism, patriotism, feelings which determine the kind of world in which we live, are rooted in very general, not carefully defined and clarified, conceptions.

What were and are prevailing views in this matter?

One of the foremost political writers of his generation and the greatest authority in the world on the question of sea power, Admiral Mahan, wrote:

> Governments are corporations, and corporations have no souls; governments, moreover, are trustees, and as such must put first the lawful interests of their wards—their own people. . . . More and more Germany needs the assured importation of raw materials, and, where possible, control of regions productive of such materials. More and more she requires assured markets and security as

to the importation of food, since less and less comparatively is produced within her own borders by her rapidly increasing population. This all means security at sea. . . . Yet the supremacy of Great Britain in European seas means a perpetually latent control of German commerce. . . . The world has long been accustomed to the idea of a predominant naval power, coupling it with the name of Great Britain, and it has been noted that such power, when achieved, is commonly often associated with commercial and industrial predominance, the struggle for which is now in progress between Great Britain and Germany. Such predominance forces a nation to seek markets, and, where possible, to control them to its own advantage by preponderant force, the ultimate expression of which is possession.[1]

Take on her side a great British soldier, the most popular of his day, Lord Roberts:

How was this Empire of Britain founded? War founded this Empire—war and conquest. When we, therefore, masters by war of one-third of the habitable globe, when *we* propose to Germany to disarm, to curtail her navy or diminish her army, Germany naturally refuses; and pointing, not without justice, to the road by which England, sword in hand, has climbed to her unmatched eminence,

[1] *The Interest of America in International Conditions.* (Sampson Low, Marston & Co., London.)

declares openly, or in the veiled language of
diplomacy, that by the same path, if by no other,
Germany is determined also to ascend! Who
amongst us, knowing the past of this nation, and
the past of all nations and cities, that have ever
added the lustre of their name to human annals, can
accuse Germany or regard the utterance of one of
her greatest a year and a half ago (or of General
Bernhardi three months ago) with any feelings
except those of respect?[2]

Take a popular British Socialist writer, Robert
Blatchford:

Why should Germany attack Britain? Because
Germany and Britain are commercial and political
rivals; because Germany covets the trade, the
Colonies, and the Empire which Britain now possesses. . . . As to arbitration, limitation of armament, it does not require a very great effort of the
imagination to enable us to see that proposal with
German eyes. Were I a German, I should say:
"These Islanders are cool customers. They have
fenced in all the best parts of the globe, they have
bought or captured fortresses and ports in five con-
tinents, they have gained the lead in commerce,
they have a virtual monopoly of the carrying trade
of the world, they hold command of the seas, and
now they propose that we shall all be brothers, and
that nobody shall fight or steal any more."[3]

[2] *Message to the Nation*, pp. 8-9.
[3] *Germany and England*, pp. 4-13.

The Editor of a pre-war monthly review:

Germany must expand. Every year an extra million babies are crying out for more room; and, as
the expansion of Germany by peaceful means seems
impossible, Germany can only provide for those
babies at the cost of potential foes. . . . She needs
the wheat of Canada, the wool of Australia . . .
which it cannot be too often repeated, is not mere
envious greed, but stern necessity. The same struggle for life and space which more than a thousand
years ago drove one Teutonic wave after another
across the Rhine and the Alps, is now once more a
great compelling force. Colonies fit to receive the
German surplus population are the greatest need
of Germany. This aspect of the case may be all
very sad and very wicked, but it is true. . . .[4]

So much for the pre-war—pre-last-war—writers.
Now let us take a few post-war present-day
writers.

A very distinguished American journalist, Mr.
Leland Stowe, a foreign correspondent attached
to the *Herald Tribune*, a man who knows Europe
and European opinion well, addressing a gather-
ing of the business *élite* of Chicago, gave expression to the prevailing view in terms which were
quite typical and which I would beg the reader
to examine with some care. Mr. Stowe said:

Terrible as it is for Mussolini to be militarizing

[4] *National Review.*

the whole people, and to have propagandized them and to set them off dropping bombs on the heads of people who have nothing but coco-nuts to return, as terrible as that is, it seems to me there is just as grave a responsibility on the shoulders of the British Government which possesses in the world more than it ever needs to have, which has taken mandates over Palestine and Iraq out of the last war as booty and a good big part of the German colonies in East Africa, and to this day has never offered to give up even 10,000 square miles to satiate either Germany or Italy in order to prevent the next war.

Nor has France offered to give up a single inch of territory in the last war. Would you say that Germany and Italy were only the ones to blame? I would say that the "haves" have just as great a responsibility as the "have-nots" for leading the whole world into this terrible thing. Until they are willing to give up something, what chance have we for peace? . . .

The nations who are the "haves" have to make up their minds to contribute something, and if France and Britain and the other nations who have the chips are not willing to play the chips, they must take part of the moral responsibility before history some day. . . .

This is only the beginning of a struggle for supremacy in the Mediterranean between Great Britain and Italy, and this struggle will go on to a showdown one way or the other. As far as the British are concerned, they will never tolerate Italy in Abyssinia. They will resort to every kind of effort, diplomatic and otherwise, to block her. If they don't block her now, and if they don't fight now, they will find a way to do it later, if possible. It is a life-and-death issue over the Mediterranean between the British and the Italians. . . .

In reality in this conflict Abyssinia is just a bone. There are two dogs after this bone, and one of them is the dog of the British Imperialism, which is very well fed and very fat, and the other is a dog of the newly-born Italian Imperialism, which is very scrawny and very hungry. That is the fundamental issue. That is why it may lead to a bigger war. . . .[5]

Note the conclusions:

The "haves" have just as great a responsibility as the "have-nots" for leading the world into "this terrible thing."

Great Britain is just as much to blame as Italy or Japan.

Britain possesses in the world more than it ever needs to have.

Britain is well fed, very fat; Italy is very scrawny, and very hungry.

Until the "haves" are willing to give up something there is no chance of peace.

Britain has refused to give even ten thousand square miles in order to prevent the next war.

[5] From an Address by Leland Stowe before the Executives' Club of Chicago, Friday, 18 October 1935.

If this does not mean that redistribution of territory is the solution, that the wealth of a people is determined by the extent of its territory, that nations with much territory are rich and nations with little territory are poor, that the world is in fact divided into poor nations which have little, and that solution of our troubles is to be found by the "haves" giving up some of their possessions to the "have-nots," so that the wealth of the world shall be divided more equitably among the nations—if the passage quoted above does not mean that, then words have no meaning.

Let us take the declarations on this point of a few European statesmen.

The Italian Ambassador in Washington declares:

> There can be no denial of the fact that we need expansion. Our forty-four million people are compressed within a territory less than half the size of your State of Texas, and not as rich in natural resources. Expansion for us is not a policy invented by Mussolini. It is a need—an actual and physical need of the Italian nation, and a need which Mussolini is trying to satisfy in order to keep the living standard of the Italian people at least at its present level; in order to prevent the restless forces of anarchy and bolshevism exploiting the hardships of an economic life which only the sound discipline of fascism has been able to make endurable.

Says Signor Grandi:

Ours is a vital problem that involves our very
existence and our future, a future of peace, tran-
quillity and work for a population of forty-two million souls, who will number fifty million in another
fifteen years. Can this population live and prosper
in a territory lacking raw materials and natural resources to meet its vital needs, pent up in a closed
sea beyond which its commerce lies, a sea the out-
lets of which are owned by other nations, while yet
others control the means of access—the Caudine
Forks of her liberty, safety, and means of livelihood
—and while all the nations of the world are raising
barriers against the development of trade, the
movement of capital, and emigration, denationaliz-
ing whoever crosses their frontiers to enter, I do not
say their own homes, but even their protectorates
and colonies?

And, finally, Mussolini himself:

The Italians are a people of workers for ever
growing in number. Italy produces more children
than coal, iron or wheat. When the needs of an
increasing population cannot be met by the scanty
resources of national territory, it follows that the
people seek expansion elsewhere. . . .
A country which has a population equal to that
of France, confined in an area half the size of the
latter, with colonial possessions one-twentieth the
size of the French and one-hundredth that of the

British, must forcibly find an outlet for her surplus inhabitants. But where and how? As it is, Italian resources hardly fill the requirements of her forty millions to-day, but the problem will become exceedingly urgent in the course of the next twenty years, when her population will have risen to fifty millions or more. At that moment Italy will find herself on the verge of servitude, certainly economic, and perhaps political.

And, of course, Hitler can never make a speech without proclaiming Germany's need for living space.

About one thousand similar quotations from politicians, Cabinet Ministers, statesmen, writers, philosophers, editors, bishops, could be given.

Now it is not the purpose of this book to explode the principal fallacies contained in all these quotations. The present writer has done that rather plentifully during the last thirty years. All he wants to do in this context is to insist that if the opinions embodied in the foregoing quotations are false, if the picture of John Bull as the fat landowner, bloated with wealth, surrounded by his landless neighbours, starving because they are landless, is a true picture, then we must face the necessity of one kind of policy, and if it is not true, face another. But the question cannot be just ignored, disregarded.

If policy is to be straight, forthright, plain, consistent, coherent, then we must answer broadly yes or no. What is the answer?

The answer is that broadly those ideas are false, that their fallacy is proved by the plain facts of the world around us.

It is not true that the welfare of a nation depends upon the extent of its territorial possessions. The people of little states, like Switzerland or Denmark, who have no empire, no "possessions," who do not demand "living space" are quite often very much richer than the people of great countries like Russia or Brazil or even Germany.

It is not true that the very real economic difficulties of Have-Not states would be solved by any device of territorial redistribution. It is true that any such remedy would create far more difficulties than it would solve. Solution indeed along the lines of territorial redistribution is impossible because you could only find "living space" for one people (e.g. Germany) by taking it from others (e.g. Poles—who have a higher birth-rate than the Germans—or Ukrainians, or Czechs, or Russians, as the case may be).

We cannot get on to the right road of solution at all until we get rid of the "possessive illusion" altogether. So long as we believe that "ownership" of Empire is possible in any real or accurate sense at all we shall wander in a jungle of confusion, a confusion related to gross inaccuracy of terms. We

talk of the British "ownership" of Canada or the
French "ownership" of Algeria. But, of course,
there is no ownership. Not a single Englishman
owns a single thing in Canada by virtue of whatever may remain of the shadowy political relationship between Britain and Canada; nor Frenchmen
a single thing in Algeria. We speak commonly as
though when a province or colony passes from one
government to another there is an actual transfer
of property or material from one group of owners
to another. But when Germany conquers Alsace
or France takes it back, there is no transfer of
"property," since the real owners are transferred
with the property. The farms, factories, houses,
shops, shares, furniture, remain in the same hands
after conquest that they were in before. There has
been a change of political administration, of government, which may be good, bad, or indifferent,
worth dying for—or dying to resist—but there is
not, properly speaking, a change of ownership.[6]

When the dispute between Great Britain and
the United States about war debts was at its
height, a certain senator proposed in the United
States Senate that Great Britain should transfer

[6] German policy in Bohemia and Poland may seem to invalidate
this argument since private property has been seized and much of
the population reduced to virtual slavery. But Germany will find,
as repeated experience of the past indicates, that slave labour is
less remunerative than free labour; and that a population in chronic
rebellion constitute an uncertain and unsatisfactory source of
wealth.

some of her property "in settlement of the debt."
He suggested the West Indies, and part of
Canada. The proposal was supported by quite a
considerable number of American newspapers.
Would there, in fact, have been a transfer of
property at all? There would have been none.
The farms, fields, factories, mines, mining shares,
houses, wireless-sets, pianos, gold teeth, would
have remained in exactly the same hands (or
mouths) after the change of flag as before. Incidentally, much of the property represented by
the bonds, debentures, mortgages, and mining
stock is already in American hands. There would
have been a change of government which, again
might be good, bad, or indifferent. There would
be no transfer of property. There would be certain economic changes. The Canadian produce,
influx of which into the United States is now regarded as so damaging to American industry, and
is excluded by tariffs, would, after annexation,
have come in without let or hindrance, and the
American producer would agitate in vain for the
imposition of tariffs by one American State against
another. The timber, beef, bacon, and butter,
which were originally considered bad economically, damaging to American forestry and farm-
ing, would suddenly, by some nationalist magic,
become good butter, timber, bacon and beef,
doing no damage to American industry. In any

case this "transfer of property" of which the senator spoke would be no transfer at all.

When Britain entered upon what so many Englishmen regarded as an utterly unjust and unnecessary war against the Boers, foreign observers commented usually that "Britain was tempted by the gold mines." But not six-pennyworth of mining shares were transferred as the result of the change of government which took place at the end of the war. And to-day, of course, the British Government has no sort of control over the mines, the acts of the British House of Commons having no validity in the South African Union.

These are not academic distinctions prompted by pedantry; they go to the very root of things when we begin to discuss cures for our troubles. The difficulties in connection with raw materials and the utilization of the world's resources for man's welfare are real and great enough in any case. It is of the utmost importance not to add to those difficulties by unnecessary confusions. A problem already refractory enough must not be made altogether insoluble by complications which are gratuitous and which a little clarity of thought and care in the use of words would avoid.

Thirty years ago the corrections of prevailing ideas advanced by this writer were regarded as great heresy, resisted even more on the Left than on the Right. They have since become quite orthodox, both on the Left and on the Right, supported by a growing body of economic literature alike in America and in Britain.[7]

As indicating the growing acceptance in America, a series of articles by Mr. Nathaniel Peffer are significant. Therein he wrote:[8]

The old faiths may die, but not the old phrases. . . . Who that has entered into the Italo-Ethiopian controversy, whether in condemnation or defence, whether cabinet minister or newspaper paragrapher, has not referred to Italy's need for expansion? The Italians say that their need for expansion compels them to make war for additional territory notwithstanding their treaty obligations. The British say that Italy's need for expansion is legitimate, but that it does not justify the violation of treaties and resort to war. None has said what need for expansion means or asked whether it means anything at all.

Need for expansion has been a potent formula in international discourse and world politics for two generations. In its name strong nations have impoverished themselves for armaments; weak nations have been crushed and primitive tribes exterminated; millions of young men have gone to their deaths in major wars, and the European continent is now apparently about to invite its own destruc-

[7] Note particularly in America the work of Professor Grover Clark of Columbia and Professor Staley of Chicago University and in Britain of Professor Robbins of London University.
[8] *Harper's Magazine.*

tion. But what is it? Exactly what does it mean? Does any country really need expansion?

"Suppose," he says, "that countries like Italy do have a 'legitimate' need to expand, what follows?"

In the first place, even on the most casual scrutiny of the sated countries satiation would not seem to be very satisfying. What nation could be more replenished than Great Britain with all that is supposed to endow a people with wealth and power and prestige? And how flourishing is Great Britain just now? How secure is its empire and how stable its economic organism? And how sweet are the fruits of world dominion to its people? In the second place, suppose Germany or even Italy should succeed in supplanting England, carving out as great an empire as the British: How much better off would it be? For an empire greater than the British no nation could hope. It is not likely that any nation can ever again be what England was in 1900, not even England. Before that can come about, nationalism will more likely have passed as a form of political and economic organization. Let the unsated redress the balance or even pull all the weights into their own scale; let them take all England's colonies and more: their needs will still not be met.

The truth is that the rewards of empire are barren in the twentieth century.

Mr. Peffer insists rightly as the conclusion from

all this that "redistribution" of resources would solve no economic problem whatsoever. If lack of "room for expansion" is at the base of economic trouble, why does Britain, with the greatest empire of history, face such grave economic difficulties, a taxation heavier than that of any other nation whatsoever? He might also have asked why, if self-sufficiency is a cure for economic distress, the United States has its present troubles.

Mr. Peffer also rightly makes the point that we shall not turn to the real solution until we have ceased to be hypnotized by these phantoms, these will-o'-the-wisps.

> Of these, the most dangerous is the belief in imperial conquest, with the glamour that has gathered round it. Empire can only lead to death and to destruction, no matter how it may be glorified by rhetoric, synthetic emotionalism and meretricious patriotism.

But until the nations see through the fallacies which buttress imperialism, they will be entrapped by its deceptions:

> Nations will arm themselves, form alliances against one another, contest with diplomatic intrigues, embark on aggressions, and finally plunge into another Armageddon, no doubt. But it should be emphasized that *they will be doing so in order to get what they will not have when they get it.*

For a long time economic writers of the Left resisted as strenuously the idea that empire did not present rich prizes for the capitalists, especially to investors: empire as a field for investment was regarded as the economic tap-root of imperialism. Even on the Left these views are being revised. The excellent little publication, *Empire*, edited by three Left writers (Mr. Leonard Barnes, Mr. J. F. Horrabin and Mr. Norman Leys), has applied to this claim the test of careful statistical investigation. It shows that the whole dependent empire brings Britain in an investment income of about £38 millions a year, which is less than one-fifth of Britain's total overseas investment income, and less than one-hundredth of her total national income. If the investment yield from all the dependent Empire were suddenly cut off, Britain's position would be like that of a man whose income was reduced from £2,000 a year to £1,980. But if Britain "lost" this Empire, there is no reason to think that such liberation would involve the loss of all the £38 millions, or indeed any part of it. The achievement of self-government by the dependencies would not necessarily, or even probably, be accompanied by the repudiation of their overseas indebtedness. It was not so accompanied when the Dominions reached their sovereign status. Why should anyone suppose it would be in the case of the dependencies? The constitu-

tional history of the British Empire tells heavily
against any such supposition.

Here is a passage from an English writer, Mr.
H. D. Dickinson, of Leeds University. Mr. Dickinson writes thus bluntly and clearly:

> The possession or non-possession of colonies has
> nothing to do with a people's poverty or wealth.
> If we classify the countries of Europe into those
> with a high standard of living and those with a low
> standard of living, we find that Britain and Hol-
> land, which have colonies, stand in the first cate-
> gory together with Denmark, Norway and Sweden,
> which have none; that Italy and Spain, which have
> no colonies to speak of, stand in the second cate-
> gory with Portugal which has colonies; that the
> Spanish people did not become poorer after 1898,
> when Spain lost her richest colonies, than they
> had been before 1898; and that the German people
> so far survived the loss of their colonies in 1919
> as to have achieved by 1928 a standard of living
> for the masses at least equal to that of victorious
> France, with all her possessions—if the German
> people are now poorer than they were it is not due
> to the enemy *outside* her gates.

But let us remember again that so long as these
ideas of "possession" are held as true, they will
have the same effect in politics as though they
were true.

But the very last conclusion we should draw

from all this is that we, the "Haves," have no obligation to the "Have-nots"; that we have merely to "stay put." We have very grave obligations to the world, and one of the main reasons for correcting false ideas concerning empire is in order to get right ideas of what ought to be done.

CHAPTER XIV

WHAT IS BRITISH IMPERIALISM?

The world, including most Britons, is still unaware that the British Empire is in process of coming to an end and turning itself into something which is not an Empire at all. Although this "de-imperialization" has been more important and significant than additions to empire, it is the feature of developments least noted by the world. Yet it gives hope of solution of the problem of imperialism.

To THE considerations presented in the last chapter one reply comes readily enough:

"If Empire is as valueless—or as little valuable —as all that why do you retain it, defend it at such cost? Perpetuate international conflict by refusing to hand back to their original rulers colonies which you say have such little worth? Why not give up your empire?"

The answer to which, of course, is first of all that we are giving up our empire—have given up most of it already. But giving it up to the people who live in it by creating independent states: that to give it up to the people living in it is a very different thing from giving it, handing it over, to nations who would make its resources a means of power to use against us; and that this is a contingency against which provision must be made, in a world where security depends, not upon the unity of the community defending each of its members, but on such individual power as each can manage in the general scramble to secure.

Two basic qualifications indeed need to be made to the statement of the foregoing chapter. The first is that though it is all true in peace time and so far as economic considerations are concerned, the case is altered in war time owing to military considerations. Empire does not give to the Briton any considerable economic advantage not possessed by the Swiss or Swede who has no empire at all. But there is a war-time advantage. The resources of our Empire then may make the difference between victory and defeat. To hand that power over to potential enemies is to demand the surrender of the strongest instinct in men, the instinct of self-preservation.

This too shows how closely the problem of inducing nations to do justice is related to the problem of affording them security; how futile it is to suppose that the first can be achieved without the second. What we term "imperialism" is generally part of that contest for power which in the present order is the condition of security and in which Soviet Russia herself has just joined.

Referring to the scramble for territory under the Secret Treaties which took place in the last war, the present author, refusing to indulge in mere invective of the wicked diplomats, tried to explain the underlying motive (particularly in reference to the promises made to Italy, which were the most outrageous of all) in these terms:

> Not only is no purpose served by making these revelations of the secret treaties the ground for railing and girding at diplomats or for indulging in recrimination, but we shall misread the real nature of the trouble by so doing. The condition of things here exposed is not due to the criminal "Imperialism" of any Ally or to the special wickedness of diplomats. The important thing to note in all these intrigues is that diplomats and peoples alike were helpless in the grip of a system. They may have had a common responsibility for the perpetuation of that system in the past. But given its existence no results other than those we have seen were possible. Even though the motives of avarice or lust of power had been entirely absent—which in the case of the Western Democracies we can well believe to be the fact—there is one justifiable and overwhelming motive which would have prompted the same policy: and that motive is national self-preservation.

He cited the case of Italy as an illustration.

> Under the system of defence by competitive power, a nation is perpetually placed in the alternative either of denying the national rights of

others or endangering its own. And under that system the better patriot and diplomat a statesman is, the more damage he does. The less entitled, in terms of nationality and international right, a country may be to a given piece of territory, the greater is the diplomatic triumph of its annexation if such annexation adds to the conqueror's national security. They are the things for which diplomats are ennobled: and they are also the things which make future wars inevitable.

Let us put it in another way.

The private road from my farm which leads to the main road is valueless to me as a source of income, a piece of property. It grows nothing, is expensive to keep up. I should be better off if it were a public highway, as I should then be relieved of all but a fraction of its upkeep, whereas now I have to assume the whole of it. I would gladly give it up to the public, under the law which would secure my right to its use.

But if my neighbour with very questionable views of public right should ask me to hand it over to him, under no law at all save his sole and irresponsible judgment as to what my rights in it would be, then I should resist to the uttermost. Though I get no income from it, though as a piece of individual property in that sense it is valueless to me, his possession of it might make my whole farm valueless by making it impossible for me to get my produce out or the goods I need.

Despite this consideration, however, the main tendency of what we call the British Empire has not been towards addition of territory as critics so readily allege. It has been towards dis-annexation, de-imperialization. If words are to have any meaning at all, the Dominions, Australia, Canada, New Zealand, South Africa, Ireland, are not "Imperial Possessions" at all. They are independent states. In a fiscal and economic sense India has already a very large measure of such independence in that she has the right to make her own tariff, and exercises that right often to the disadvantage, the very considerable disadvantage, of British traders, manufacturers and capitalists.

But to hand over the government of territory to the people who really "own" it, the people who live there, is very different indeed from handing over its government to other alien rulers. The first process means making a beginning in getting rid of imperialism; the second means perpetuating imperialism by splitting it into a larger number of rival and competing imperialisms. De-imperialization, which Britain has already carried so far, is incompatible with the policy of self-sufficient empires, a world of economic nationalism. The German proposals are based on the policy of national or imperial self-sufficiency.

The issue is much more than economic. It profoundly affects the political problem of defence, security. No method of defence compatible with peace is possible if nations insist upon national self-sufficiency. We shall find on examination that the methods of defence which we adopt are largely determined by the view we take of the "struggle for bread" problem; and that the adoption of the current view of "need for expansion" prevents any solution of the purely political problem.

§

Why did the British Empire cease to be an Empire properly speaking, and resolve itself, in large part, into a loose alliance of practically independent states? Why did the Mother Country surrender the economic privileges of an imperial position in according fiscal autonomy to its daughter states? No other empire in the past has done this. Spain did not, nor Portugal, nor Holland.

The evolution, alike on its political and economic sides, has exceedingly interesting and significant aspects. If we cut beneath words and symbols to the underlying reality we see that there has taken place, what we have been assured again and again by students of politics never could take place—changes of frontier, the creation of new

frontiers, without war. Communities, originally
part of an empire, have achieved a separate political status "in no way subordinate" to that of the
states of which originally they were part. That is
to say, frontiers have been changed. There are
states, independencies and sovereignties where
originally none existed; and this thing has been
produced without war. The independence for
which the Thirteen Colonies had to fight is ac-
corded to Canada even without bitterness. Territory is freely "given up."

But why did we so readily acquiesce, so readily
surrender our power, more especially power over
the fiscal policies of the component territories of
the Empire? What are the motives behind this
process of economic "de-imperialization"? The
surrender of economic control in the territories
we have conquered?

While so much attention has been directed to
exposing the capitalist roots of imperialism, very
little attempt seems to have been made to explain,
in terms of economic motive, the capitalist retire-
ment from imperialism, the process by which vast
territories like Australia, New Zealand, Canada,
the Cape, the Philippine Islands, have passed out
of the control of the imperial powers which originally conquered them, have ceased to be in matters economic imperial territory, and have become
economically independent states. Arrangements

like those made at Ottawa are not in the nature of privileges imposed upon reluctant subject-provinces by an imperial centre in London for the benefit of the Mother Country in the manner of the sixteenth-century Spanish Empire, but are bargains made between equally sovereign nations, in which the Dominion of Great Britain does not necessarily come off best.

The economic importance of the area which, during the last sixty or seventy years, has become de-imperialized, "unconquered," is infinitely greater than that of the area of fresh conquests. Yet while the economically less important has been the subject of a vast amount of attention of the kind described, the more important has been all but completely ignored.

In important and pretentious books authorities write as though this astonishing change had never taken place at all. I take at hazard a few passages from American books, though something similar could be found in English.

Mr. Frederic Bausman, a Federal Judge of the Supreme Court of Washington, in his book, *Facing Europe*, writes:

So extensive is the British Empire's possession of raw materials that it is hardly likely she will long remain poor; and for that matter it is not in a military sense that Britain is poor to-day, since she still can wield that mightiest of weapons, the dominating navy of the world. . . .

From India, from Australia, from South Africa, and from Canada, her sons returned laden with the profits of newly-developed regions. Proprietorship of those regions was thus bringing back its gains. . . .

After a bloody war in which Germany has barely escaped the jaws of Russia, Great Britain emerges in practical control of Persia, and in absolute control of rich Mesopotamia, once the granary of the world, easily made again its granary, and fabulously rich in oil. . . .

The tentacles of England extend everywhere, from Halifax to Jamaica, from London to Capetown, from Gibraltar to Siam; and those tentacles have a sensitive power of suction.

One of the publications (date 1935) of the American Foreign Policy Association which exists to put the facts of the international situation before the American public, explaining a chart showing the difference in possessions between the "haves" and the "have-nots," says:

The war to end war failed to solve the economic problems that had been its root cause. For back of national jealousies and desire for power is always the pressure for more territory, greater resources, increasing world markets. The chart shows the population of the leading nations, and how much wheat, potatoes, coal, steel, oil and cotton they produced in 1933. . . .

The chart shows why England has built up a great empire of colonies from whom she can import the things she lacks and to whom she can send surplus population and production. . . .[1]

Thus easily do these old conceptions cause serious writers to slip into sheer misstatement of fact. The statement that Britain can send her surplus goods and population to the Empire implies, of course, that Britain has the power to dictate to the component states of the Empire whether or not their tariffs shall exclude British goods and their immigration laws British people. It would be truer to say that Britain has no more power to impose, to dictate the tariffs or immigration laws of the Dominions than she has those of the United States. She may bargain with the Dominions as she may bargain with Argentina or Denmark, but the last word does not rest with her—as those who live by certain British industries interested in

[1] The statement goes on: Germany is densely populated, produces little wheat, many potatoes, some coal, a little steel, practically no oil and no cotton. She now has no colonies. It is easy to see why she is accused of looking with envious eyes at the Russian Ukraine, rich in agriculture and mineral deposits. There the famous black soil belt yields large crops of wheat, sugar beet and oil seeds. There in the Donetz Basin are vast deposits of coal, iron and other metals. There, too, are large chemical and dye industries, salt mines and newly-developed electric power plants.

Dominion markets have very good cause to know. The statement about population is particularly significant. There is no part of the Empire suitable for white colonists where British citizens can now go as of right; no area from which British subjects at times when emigration is most necessary—in times of depression that is—are not excluded as rigidly as they are excluded from any foreign country.

This same notion of Britain as the "possessor" of an estate was often the theme of so distinguished a writer as the late Frank D. Simonds. In a map which he publishes in one of his works, *Price of Peace,* which was also published in *The Strategy of Raw Materials,* Canada, Australia, New Zealand, South Africa, are all marked as British "possessions," the raw materials of which "belong to Britain." In one of Simonds's articles occurs the passage:

> With growing populations hammering at narrow frontiers the "have-nots" look forward to the day when their field-marshals and admirals will lead them to victories that will win the territories they covet. . . . Ultimately the "haves" must give the "have-nots" the land they need, or in the end they must fight to prevent them from taking it.

A double illusion is, of course, involved in the foregoing: (a) the illusion that any nation needs to "possess," to have within its political borders in peace-time the raw materials of its industry (as though Britain had not built her greatest export trade, the cotton trade of Lancashire, upon a foreign raw material, and as though she had to "conquer" Louisiana or Georgia in order to render its products available for British use), and (*b*) the illusion concerning the nature of the British Empire.

In perpetuating this latter illusion the use of the old names and symbols does undoubtedly play a part. If the South African Union called itself "the South African Republic" or "the United States of South Africa," its resources would never have been marked on any map as "belonging" to Britain. These misconceptions are momentarily important in the international field. The demand that the "haves" surrender something of their "possessions" to the "have-nots" would lose a good deal of its force if it were fully realized that the "haves" do not for the most part possess what they "have" and consequently cannot well give it up.

The reference to Ottawa brings up the second qualification to be made to the considerations advanced in the previous chapter: our attempts at Empire Preference. The process of de-imperialization there sketched is accompanied by a contrary tendency to empire trade monopoly, although Preferences are not imposed by an imperium in London but are a matter of bargain. They are of most dubious benefit to the peoples of the Empire and all based largely upon fallacy; but from that fallacy foreigners suffer. Although our Preferences may not benefit us, they certainly do make the position of foreigners more difficult. They must be brought to an end and in the final chapter of this book the simplest and directest way of doing it is indicated.

§

When in September 1935, it looked as though Britain were intent upon putting her power behind the policy of sanctions in order to stop the Italian war in Abyssinia, I happened to be in the United States, and almost everywhere, particularly among those of the Left, of Radical tendencies, did one hear something like this:

Now we shall see Britain at last really champion of the League and become eloquent about her righteousness. For this move of Britain's in the matter of sanctions is, of course, merely a clever bit of imperialism. She means to stop Italy going into Abyssinia in order that later she may take it for herself. That is why Britain declared her policy to be a League policy: it enables her to grab more and more territory and keep others out of it. Of course, it is not merely an Abyssinian question:

British Imperialism could never swallow Italian command of the Eastern Mediterranean threatening the Imperial "life line" through the Suez to India, the Antipodes, the East. Oh! Now we shall see how Holy has the League become and with what passion Britain will uphold it.

Anyone who cares to refer to the American Press of that date will find columnists, letter-writers, leader-writers, all commenting in those terms and being very realist, cynical, hard-boiled about it; and all done with a very knowing air of "You can't fool us."

It was quite useless to point out that all those who really knew the situation in Britain had become convinced that the British Government would not apply sanctions in any such way as really to hamper Italy; that British imperialists of the traditional order were bitterly opposed to sanctions and were daily expressing their desire to see Italy triumphant; that the support of sanctions did not come from the imperialist end of British politics at all, but from the Left, alike in Britain, in France and among the neutrals; that while all the fire-eating colonels and imperialists were disparaging and deriding the League and praising Italy, the Labour Party, the Socialists, the Communists, the small states in the League— including Ireland and Mr. de Valera personally— who had most to fear from imperialism, strongly supported League action as against the British imperialist. But it was all no good. Those critics instead continued to insist that a policy opposed by all British imperialists and supported by all anti-imperialists, was nothing but pure British imperialism.

The reason for American scepticism, of course, was that the assertion that British imperialists were undermining the power of the Empire simply did not make sense. It was easier to have a simple issue, and behaviour that conformed to the familiar, conventional, pre-conceived pattern. It is related that during the last war a number of American correspondents, including photographers, were received by Foch in a room in the War Ministry. The photographers were to be allowed to take pictures. But several of the photographers gasped: there were no maps on the wall, and as everyone knows a great general should be surrounded by maps. "But why?" asked Foch, on the point being explained to him. "If I want a map I send to the cartographer's room; I don't keep them here." No good. A general's room must have maps on the wall; readers must be given what they expect to see or read, not unexpected versions of preconceived situations. They demand the familiar, the simple, the understood.

But British imperialism is not as simple as that and it was precisely the feature of the situation which the American critics refused to look at which was the most significant, the most pregnant.

That the British Government did not really intend to make sanctions effective, to take any risks of collision with Italy in so doing, has been made perfectly clear by many historians: among them Mr. Winston Churchill. And British policy in respect of the Abyssinian episode is characteristic of British policy throughout a long series of retreats, each one of which grievously weakened its imperial position and made any stand against the next retreat less likely because a stand would be the more difficult and risky.

The allegation of "imperialist motives" seems to fly in the face of at least the most obvious facts. It would be entirely true to say this:

If Britain had "used" the League to maintain her own imperial position; had with that view taken risks to maintain the League's authority, not only would the League now be a strong and vital institution, but we should not now be at war.

The more discerning critics in the extreme left do not now indeed take the position of the American critics above referred to. Their argument runs—and it had become a very familiar one in Left circles—that all along the political Right in Britain has been sacrificing the interests of the Empire to the interests of their class; that they supported Mussolini in Abyssinia because his defeat might so weaken his position at home that his government and regime might collapse and be followed by a Socialist or Communist one. So in Spain: they would rather place the communications of the Empire in mortal jeopardy by risking the domination of the Peninsular by Italy and Germany than see established there a Socialist or Communist government. That argument is re-enforced, of course, enormously by the history of the relations with Russia. Although it was admitted that the presence of Russia was indispensable to a Peace Front sufficiently strong to deter Hitler, an admission implicit in the negotiations which were opened with Russia early in 1939, those negotiations (allege the critics) were conducted with such indifference, such lack even of decent civility, were marked by such delays and hesitations that they broke down; the breakdown precipitating war, and vast dangers to the Empire. Rather that, argued the Right, rather dire peril to our national and imperial existence than "shaking hands with murder" and the spread of Bolshevism.

I have always regarded this Marxist explanation as inadequate and much over-simplified. But such element of truth as it has—and it has some, if not a good deal—is itself proof that the motives behind the war are not "imperialist," a sheer desire to preserve and enlarge the Empire. Quite clearly other motives have not only entered in, they have swamped the instinct of imperialist self-protection.

Recently, in a course of lectures delivered to foreign universities, the extent of ignorance as to what was taking place in the Empire (not perhaps much greater than that sometimes displayed in England itself) was brought home very vividly to this present writer. A questioner would seek to explain or justify the conduct of Germany or Italy by the density of the "Have-not" population. I would point out that the density of population in England and Wales was just about twice what it is in (say) Italy. The retort would come immediately: "Oh, but you have the whole of the Empire to go to." Did the questioner then think that it was open to Britain to send her unemployed as she wished into Canada and Australia? Why, yes, of course. Did the questioner think that the immigration laws of Canada or Australia were made by the British Parliament and Government? Equally, of course. I might even get a disquisition on the British Constitution: All Bills, in every British Parliament, had to have the Royal assent, and the King would certainly withhold assent if the Bill were inimical to British interest. Usually the questioners—educated, many engaged in the study of political science—have never heard of the Statute of Westminster. If its purport were explained they were quite sure there was a catch in it somewhere. And if, to cut argument short, I declared that Britain had no more power to vary the immigration restrictions of Australia or Canada than she had to vary those of the United States, I was met with quite open disbelief based on the line of argument, "It could not be true because if it were true it would be absurd."

All this ground has been covered in previous works of the present author. It is necessary to recall the facts in this context because the ideas which the facts deny are held with obstinacy that marks a determination not to surrender a familiar conception in favour of a less familiar, and one which demands some readjustment of ideas.

One last point in this connection should be considered as it bears upon the question of "League or Federalism," dealt with in the next chapter.

The argument for Federalism is that a League of Nations must fail because it is merely a League of Governments. But the British Commonwealth is a League of Governments and it has not taken the federal line because even in the case of states having such deep, common, historical roots as those of the Commonwealth, the impulse of localism, local independence, the magic of the word "independence" and the easy growth of such vested interests as flourish behind tariff walls, have all so far resisted the efforts towards federalism.

But those foreign or domestic critics of the rapacity of British Imperialism in holding on to such possessions as South Africa, or Canada, or Eire, and who demand instead a federation of all democracies, seem rather to overlook that federation would demand an immeasurably greater surrender of independence or autonomy than the presence of South Africa, or Australia, or even India within the Empire has demanded. The nations of the Commonwealth would have far less self-government in any system of world federation than they have as members of the British Commonwealth. Indeed, more than one writer has pointed out that the bonds which tie the nations of the Commonwealth together at Geneva are at least formally tighter than those which tie them at Westminster.

CHAPTER XV

PLANNING FOR THE FUTURE

There is no lack of beautiful blue prints: "perfect plans"; the difficulty is to induce men to work them. Fallacies, illusions, prejudices, vested interests stand in the way. Those obstacles must be cleared out of the way if any plan at all is to work.

How may unification of the West be best achieved?

Nothing is easier than to lay down a perfect plan, a blue print, that shall be beyond reproach. That has never been the trouble. As a French monarch said when such a plan of European peace was shown him: "It is indeed perfect. I can see no single fault in it. Save this: No earthly prince would ever dream of being guided by it."

Our plans must always, therefore, be compromises between what would be the best arrangement if men were politically wise, and what they will accept: some plan demanding less change of present habit and outlook would nevertheless put us on the road which leads at last in the direction of our objective, so that as we go along we may quicken our pace.

The League has had many critics, but they have

not yet agreed as to what was wrong with it. They are divided broadly into two categories—those who say that it asked far too much of men, and nations, and those who think that it asked far too little; those, that is, who think that it should have been a consultative body, devoting itself mainly to social work, health services, labour office, and so forth, leaving the problem of defence, security, alone; and those who believe that it could only effectively tackle the problem of defence by an economic and political federalism approximating to that of the states in the American Union.

I have yet to meet anyone actually concerned with the initiation of the League of Nations and the drafting of its Covenant (and it has been my fortune to meet most of those who were), who would agree that there was the most distant likelihood of the nations concerned at that time surrendering their sovereignty and independence to any such degree as the states of the American Union have surrendered theirs to the federal government. Even the tentative measures of the federal type advocated by the present writer at that time (the proposals are reproduced at the end of this chapter) failed of general support or even attention. Certainly the world was not ready for so great a step.

Will it be possible to take it on the morrow of this war?

No one, of course, can possibly tell. It is quite impossible to be positive concerning future changes in public outlook and feeling. The recent performances of the German and the Russian publics respectively in that connection illustrate how malleable opinion and feeling are, what sweeping changes of attitude can be made from one day to another. And, as some of the preceding pages have shown, our own and American opinion, have shown somersaults hardly less strange.

What one can say, in the light of experience, in respect of the public attitude to peace plans is this: Even if you got agreement (as you got enthusiastic support by the American public for the League) to a plan of Federal Union, that plan would share the fate of the American agreement to the League unless certain precedent conditions were fulfilled.

Those conditions relate to the understanding by the public of the reasons for the change: a real sense of its need.

Every generous plan that promises a way out from the horrors, any medicine that promises to cure our disease, can count upon enthusiastic support from certain groups and agreement from far wider sections, based on the attitude "it may be worth a trial." But if that assent is secured without adequate understanding of what the patient has to do, the support will prove worthless when

it comes to doing the things necessary for cure.
The patient will then decide, especially if the
worst phases of the horrors are over, as America
decided after the war, that perhaps the cure was
worse than the disease.

Any move in the direction of federalism will
most certainly fail if we deem that it is unnecessary to explode the fallacies which now buttress
the obstacles that federalism would have to overcome.

Take two points, tariffs and restrictions of immigration. Not merely during the last few years,
but during the last half-century, economic nationalism has been one of the strongest forces in international affairs. When depression comes the first
device to which nations resort is the increase of
their tariff against their neighbours. All the genuine sentiment that lies behind the conception of
the British Commonwealth of Nations has not
been sufficient even to attenuate this tendency to
economic exclusions and restrictions. The tariffs
of one British Dominion against another have
grown as much as the tariffs of the separate non-
British states of the world each against the other.
All the crusades for Empire free trade, for making
the British Empire an economic unit have broken
themselves upon the hard rock of economic nationalism. Every Dominion, when war comes, is
prepared to die for the Empire, to give her sons.

None of them so far has been prepared to give those tariffs, or any considerable part of them, to make an economically consolidated empire.

The cause of economic federalism is not hopeless, but it can only be tackled by what must ultimately be an educational process, by a systematic hammering at simplifications and the destruction of certain fallacies for the benefit of the great public; a simplification which most economists seem to dislike.

So with immigration. Only those who have struggled with such issues as those involved in the refugee problem during the last few years understand the fierce feeling which blocks any considerable lessening of the restrictions. Federalism would demand almost certainly that the restrictions be swept away.[1]

The restrictions are based, particularly in the case of nations of stationary or declining population, on considerations that are almost entirely completely fallacious. The fallacy does not weaken the intensity with which they are held.

One trap at the outset should be avoided. Terms such as League, Federal Union, are not absolute. Federalism may take infinite forms, varying from the very loose gentleman's agreement form of federalism, a federalism applicable only to de-

[1] See *You and the Refugee* by Norman Angell and Dorothy F. Buxton. And also note at the end of Chapter IX herewith.

fence, which characterizes the British Common-
wealth, and the intensely centralized form of the
U.S.S.R., in which nearly all power is held by
Moscow, though in form it is a Union of Separate
Republics. Between these two are an infinitely
varying degree of unification.

What is the essential difference between League
and Federation?

The distinction is not made clear at all by saying that a League is an alliance of sovereign states,
designed to perpetuate and safeguard the sovereignty of its members. For no League can exist
unless its members surrender some degree of sovereignty. If the League obligations had been taken
seriously, especially those relating to defence,
there would have been a very considerable qualification alike of independence and sovereignty.
Had this nascent constitution been worked with
genuine desire to make the most of it, and to bring
it as much as possible to a real federation, it could
quickly have developed in that direction. Federation would have grown out of the basic principle
of mutual assistance for purposes of defence. But
we have seen what happened to that, in the case
of Britain and France. The foregoing pages have
shown that the first grievous renunciation of that
principle by Britain was not either in the case of
Manchuria, or Abyssinia, or Czecho-Slovakia. It
was repudiated first of all in the case of France,

owing mainly to the confusions in the public mind. Those confusions were due largely to the hypnotism of names. The guarantees for which France asked constituted an "alliance" with her and "alliances" were, we argued, evil and dangerous things. It was hopeless to try to get across the fact that it makes all the difference in the world what an alliance is for—whether to uphold law or defy it; whether the alliance is of a kind which is open to those against whom it is directed or one to which they must submit or fight.

Anti-German passion accounted for much evil. Early admission of Germany into the League was refused because "You could not trust Germany," the whole problem being, of course, to induce Germany to trust us.

The list of similar confusions could be extended indefinitely; many of them have been dealt with in the preceding pages.

The mere fact of having had a constitution more federal in character would not have swept away these confusions. And until they had been, a more federal constitution would merely have made the gap between the paper arrangements and what men and women were really feeling, more apparent than ever. Such a Covenant would have been as little effective for security and order as are some of the very beautiful and perfect constitutions of certain Spanish American Republics who for generations never managed to survive a single year without a revolution of some kind.

Nearly all federal constitutions embody this dual principle, namely that there shall be representation not only of the states, members of the union, but of the people themselves who form those states. All federal union is a union of individuals and peoples, as well as of governments and states.

It is a very important principle, and when the League of Nations appeared on the horizon during the Great War, as a possibility of the future, this present writer urged that this principle of popular as well as of governmental representation should be embodied in its constitution. He realized that the introduction of such a principle would have to be tentative, experimental, but he made several suggestions to that end. In outline, his suggestions amounted to this:

If we are to have a League, let us, while the war is on, make a real League of the Allies themselves, for if the Grand Alliance which fights the war goes to pieces, the victory itself will be impermanent. He went on, moreover, to suggest that with the ferment set up by the revolution of 1917, there should be found, in such a League of the Allies, some means of representing political parties other than those who happened to have obtained

possession of the government. Otherwise we were
not in fact talking with the nations at all.

At that time—in 1918—the allied governments
seemed to be in mortal terror of minorities within
their own states, of "infection" from Russia. The
present author's book, which appeared in that
year, has these notes of constructive suggestions,
which are reprinted since they are about as apposite to conditions to-day as they were then.
Here they are:

A FEDERAL SUGGESTION FROM 1918

The only effect of depriving minority opinion,
whether in Britain, France, Italy, or Russia, of any
real representation in international "official" bodies
is to drive that opinion to extra-governmental representation, as in Socialist and Labour Conferences. And the only effect of forbidding those
Conferences is to intensify the sense of grievance
among the minorities—destined to-morrow perhaps
to be majorities—and to create a disunion which
some unforeseen circumstance may render dangerous. The unifying method would be to provide for
constitutional representation of those minorities in
the international field. The absence in our present
machinery for handling international affairs, of
anything in the nature of a European legislature or
deliberative assembly, where the opposition parties
in the States of our Alliance could express themselves, renders it inevitable that complex democ-

racies should be represented by governments chosen for purely administrative purposes and out of touch with what may be the prevailing aims of their peoples. Real unity of the Western Democracies cannot come from such conditions.

We should realize the extent to which the major motives in international politics are shifting from the political to the economic or social ground; and the extent to which such a change renders obsolete our present methods of handling international affairs—the method which necessarily assumes each of the geographical areas we call "nations" to be a political, social or moral unit.

The world is not yet in a position to interpret the Russian revolution—to know even what took place. But among a mass of uncertainties a few things are certain.

First, that though the political ideals of the Western Democracies are much more in sympathy with those of the Russian revolution than are those of Germany, it is German diplomacy which has made most efficient use of the moral factors in the Russian situation; and secondly, our failure to make equivalent use of those factors has been due in large part to the situation created by our recourse to the old diplomacy and the consequent entanglements of the secret treaties.

M. Cheradame, the French publicist, declares that the disruption of Russia "was brought about, not by force of arms but by means of a moral propaganda, carried on by speech or in print." But why was Germany alone able to carry on this propaganda? We had not only the more democratic cause but for the three years of our Alliance we had a facility and openness of access denied after all to the Germans. Here were two factors in our favour, yet the German effort succeeded and ours failed.

We know now the salient which was left open to German attack in this moral struggle for the capture of the Russian political soul. For reasons just indicated the mass of Russians, inspired with a new social and economic vision, and having themselves renounced territorial aggrandizement and "imperialist" aims, were not ready to jeopardize the revolution and its aims by a long-continued war on behalf of what the Germans alleged to be (and which we did not sufficiently counter) a policy of European imperialism, the very success of which would spell the defeat of all that was vital and real to them in the revolutionary programme. The starting-point of the German propaganda in Russia, to which M. Cheradame refers, was the suggestion: "The Allied aims are imperialistic; their success will make your revolutionary aims impossible of realization." Hints as to the nature of the secret treaties were freely scattered. Already under Miliukoff one heard the demand "publish the secret treaties." The effective counter to the German propaganda would have been to show the falseness of the assertion upon which it was based.

Kerensky made it plain that in order to hold Russia even passively to the Alliance, there would have to be a restatement of aims which would clearly show the parties of the Left that the Alliance was not fighting for an imperialist Europe that would make a socialist Russia impossible.

Why was that clear restatement of aims, despite many promises, never made by the Allies?

The nature of the secret treaties—and it cannot be too often and too insistently pointed out that those treaties were fully justified by the needs of the national security of the nations involved, so long as nothing better than the old Balance of Power scheme of Europe could be devised—sufficiently supplied the answer.

Events have in some measure compelled us to recognize what evidently was not clear before, that though the power of the Alliance obviously depends, not merely upon the military forces of each constituent state, but also upon the capacity to combine those forces for a common purpose, collective unity cannot be taken for granted. We may unintentionally develop a policy bound to destroy it.

We have seen already that unity is impossible by the old methods of statecraft and diplomacy; and that the only alternative is for nations to cease their competition for individual power one with another, and trust for their security instead to co-operation for reciprocal protection. But such a method, being only a project, an aspiration, a "dream," no one regards it as reliable or feasible; so each falls back upon competition for territory and power, which provokes instability within the groups, and thus makes the general agreement still more remote. Our scepticism sets up the very conditions which we cite as its justification.

The ultimate fact in our problem, therefore, is a moral one. The chief obstacles to the abolition of the old disintegrating policy and the success of the new, are not mainly physical, like difficulty of communication over wide distance (which mechanical development has in large measure met), but moral and intellectual difficulties, the mental habits, opinions, and impulses of men, which have not kept pace with the changes wrought by our progress in mechanical contrivance. Our management of matter has altogether outstripped our management of human relationships, of our own minds and natures.

Yet that the moral forces are capable of change we have the testimony not only of those who desire the change, but of those who do not.

We are dealing with two currents of feeling and opinion: the old impulses and feelings of nationalism, at present controlling governments; and the newer social and economic forces, menacing governments; both make for the disintegration of our Alliance, and, partly at least, for the integration of the enemy.

What are the practical steps of policy to meet these conditions?

Let us take the political side of the problem first.

The proposals here made to meet the political situation of the Alliance are:

(1) The transformation of our Alliance into a permanent League of Nations in which two main principles shall operate: (*a*) That the security of each state should rest upon the combined strength of the whole League. (*b*) That the League shall offer to the enemy peoples this clear alternative: Admission into the League on equal terms and *protection by it*, on conforming to its conditions (which may include democratic representation in foreign affairs); or, on failure to conform to its conditions exclusion from the benefits of the League, and, instead, the penalty of such coercive measures, economic and other, which it can employ.

(2) The mechanism of such a League should provide not merely for the representation of its constituent states as geographical units and national or political entities, but (by proportional representation) of the minority parties therein.

The Constitution of this Preparatory Inter-Allied Congress should itself, conform to the principle of representing peoples as well as governments, and, for the purpose of formulating the plan of the Society of Nations, consist of two bodies: a smaller one, composed, as in international congresses of the past, of the delegates or nominees of the executive branches of the governments represented, and a larger body drawn from the legislatures of such governments, and not only from the majority

parties, but, proportionately from the minority, opposition, parties as well.

The smaller body might act as the initiating and
drafting committee, their proposals being subject
to the discussion, amendment, and even rejection
of the legislative representatives, before being
finally ratified by the constituent states of the Congress. The discussions of this larger body should
of course be public.

The Allied nations should make it known that
they stand in common for this method of representation as the basic principle of the final peace
Congress whenever that takes place.

The reasons for urging that method are mainly
two:

(1) It is indispensable to our own unification.

(2) It is indispensable to the democratization of
Germany in foreign affairs—the only practical
method of carrying into effect our policy of not
dealing with the German autocracy.

It will be noted that territorial questions are at
this stage excluded. The reason for that is to be
found in almost every argument in these pages.
Until the problem of national security and economic
opportunity has been met, the territorial conflicts
are insoluble. "Since your League of Nations is not
a reality, I must have this strategic alien province,
it is necessary to my defence; that province, because it contains ore. Annexation violates the principle of nationality, but you cannot ask for our
suicide on behalf of the political ideals of other

people." Until national sovereignty and independence, are qualified by certain international rules,
to do justice to one party will be to do injustice to
another: the security of one makes the insecurity
of the other.

Everything so far urged points to this one great
need: the making of the plan of a Society of Nations
a present reality. How can our democracies co-
operate in that except by some such method as an
Inter-Allied Congress?[2]

[2] *The Political Conditions of Allied Success.*

CHAPTER XVI

CONCLUSION: WHAT WE MUST DO AND WHY

If stalemate on the West continues, it can be turned to our advantage for building, behind the defences of the French Maginot Line, and British command of the sea, a nucleus Western unity of strongly attractive power to the neutrals by reason of the economic advantages and political securities it can offer them; one calculated also to stimulate the right kind of revolution in Germany, and to meet the peculiar conditions created by the rising power of Russia. Whether this Western unification (which alone can meet the challenge of Russo-German Totalitarianism) comes into being, will depend less upon the precise form of the constitution, than upon the degree of public wisdom that can be applied to its working; whether repetition of the old errors can be avoided.

THIS war rose because we promised to defend Poland, and proceeded to implement that promise. We gave that promise because we—France and Britain—realized that if aggression continued unchecked, we (like all Western Europe) would be at the complete mercy of an authority whose domination and sovereignty means what it has meant in Vienna and in Prague. If piecemeal destruction of lesser states by the Nazi power went on, there would be an end in Europe of the kind of life which we of the West have learned to value.

How do we propose to restore the independence of Poland, Czecho-Slovakia, Austria, and make their independence secure in view of what has happened? We established those States, together with others, under the ægis of victors who had achieved the complete defeat and submission of Germany. Twenty years later we see those States destroyed by the erstwhile defeated enemy. If we defeat him again, and set up those States again, how long will their independence last if we proceed after the next war as we proceeded after the last?

Indeed, we must ask, what "victory" and "defeat" will mean in the light of the new military conditions of enormously powerful permanent entrenchment and fortification on both sides; of highly-developed air arms and of a diplomatic situation in which France and Britain having exhausted themselves in the defeat of Germany are confronted with a fresh and unexhausted Russia.

Russia now occupies the eastern half of Poland, strategic points on the territories of the Baltic States, has once more acquired a great sphere of influence in the Balkans, is on intimate terms with Turkey, is rapidly growing in power, and has a much larger population increase than Western Europe. If present population trends persist, some now living will see a France of twenty millions, a Britain of twenty-five millions, and a highly-developed Russia of six hundred millions.

Yet the aim which we proclaimed on entering the war was the defence of Poland. We are therefore pledged to its restoration in some form. But if we are to restore Poland to the Treaty of Riga frontiers, then, having defeated Germany, we should have to defeat Russia, since Russia is now in occupation of a large part of that Poland. Obviously we are not going to fight Russia for the purpose of restoring Polish frontiers which had no basis in anything but the temporary power of the Polish Army. The frontiers in which Poland has lived since the Treaty of Riga were not fixed by the Allies, or by impartial authority. They were the results of military *faits accomplis.*

One motive entering into British and French policy of the last twenty years has been fear of the spread of Bolshevism. It was this motive which caused the Allies so readily to acquiesce in Polish territorial conquests in the early days of the post-war settlement. And it was this motive also—very frankly avowed at the time—which lay behind the creation of the seaboard Baltic States. They and Poland were to form what Clemenceau described as the *cordon sanitaire* against the Bolshevist infection of Europe. But the present war between the Western Allies and Germany, and the firm establishment of Russian power in the eastern half of Poland, and strategically in the Baltic States, has produced this situation: the more that the power of Germany is weakened by British and French assaults upon it, the greater relatively does the power of Russia become. To the degree to which we withdraw German power from the East in order to meet our pressure upon the West wall of Germany, the greater become the opportunities of Russia to penetrate into areas heretofore marked out for German sphere of influence, and, indeed, by doctrinal penetration, into Germany itself. We look upon revolution of the German people against the present German regime as one of the objectives of the war. But the character of that revolution may well be determined far more by Russia than by ourselves. The net result of Conservative and Reactionary hostility to Bolshevism has been greatly to increase the power of Russian Bolshevism, and the area of its direct domination.

The attempt to force Russia out of territories which are more Russian than Polish would result in the creation of a Russo-German alliance which we would have to defeat.

§

How do we propose to turn Germany out of Western Poland, Bohemia and Austria?

In 1918 the German Army collapsed because,

after withstanding for three years the assaults of
the Russian, the French, the British, the Belgian,
and for a lesser period the Italian and Roumanian
forces; a complete blockade, virtually on all sides,
she had to face after those strains, the power of
the United States. Internal exhaustion—the effect
of hunger on the civil population, a shortage of
necessary material for the military forces—was a
large factor.

To-day Germany is entrenched behind a series
of Siegfried Lines, assaults upon which would be
far more exhausting to those attacking than to
those defending, and hopes to draw upon the
resources of Russia, in whose technical development German technicians propose to take a large
part.

The Siegfried Lines may not be theoretically
impregnable. To break through them would involve a cost which would indeed bleed France—
of declining population—very white indeed, and
leave Britain little better. There is probably no
sane military authority on either side who proposes frontal attack upon the fortified lines of the
other. There is in that area stalemate.

To the stalemate of the two confronting lines
of impregnable fortifications and entrenchment
has to be added another kind of stalemate which
results from the preceding considerations. That

stalemate expresses itself, up to the time of writing, in an unspoken and unwritten convention that while air forces can be used against military lines, against warships, they shall not be used in such a way as to involve wholesale civilian devastation. Both sides, for all the reasons indicated, have an interest in maintaining that convention: Hitler because civilian chaos would open the way to revolution of a kind which might turn against him, and France and Britain because they, no more than Hitler, want to see a Bolshevist Germany arising out of the ruins which Totalitarian air warfare might produce in Germany—to say nothing of the devastation of their own countries, which would also help to give the last word to Stalin.

What might bring that convention to an end would be a German conquest of Holland and Belgium, enabling Germany to make their territories her real air bases, as well as main bases for submarine action. Those conquests would place Germany in such a favourable position for air action, and us in so unfavourable a one for retaliation, that she would then be tempted to secure decision by air *"blitzkrieg."*

Decision by the air arm could not be purchased save at a cost of very great disorganization of civil life on both sides. Let us assume that Germany

suffers most in an air duel to the death, and that
her vital processes or activities—industries, rail-
ways, electrical plants, water systems, communications—are so paralysed that the revolution we
speak of so much begins to take place. France and
Britain (as well as Germany) will also have been
weakened by the strain of the duel, although definitely preponderant. But Russia will have been
facing no such strain (always assuming her continued neutrality), and will be in a very powerful
position, as we have seen, to direct the course of
the German revolution, to aid one side or the other
in that revolution. Will she just stand aside and
let the revolution go Right or Left without any
sort of interference or intervention?

What we may expect from Hitler, the arch op-
portunist, at such a moment is just that development which so many have predicted—acquiescence in the conversion of the Nazi revolution
into a Bolshevist revolution. Hitler would be denying all his past behaviour (though not his past
words) if he did not take the initiative in that
situation, and anticipate any movement against
himself either from the monarchist Right, or the
Liberal social-democracy, by coming to a still
closer bargain with Stalin. We should then be
confronted with a Bolshevization of Germany—
as the outcome of a policy on the part of France

and Britain which had been animated largely by
a fear and hatred of Bolshevism.

§

Military science has often been criticized by
its more clear-headed exponents as suffering from
an almost ineradicable tendency to "get ready for
past wars"; to assume, that is, that the next war
will in fact be like the last. Our preparations for
a peace settlement seem to be suffering from a
similar tendency, from the assumption that the
conditions of the next settlement will be pretty
much like the last, where a completely defeated
Germany is hailed to the Hall of Mirrors in Versailles, and where in consequence we shall be
able to lay down freely the frontiers and conditions of the new Poland, the new Czecho-Slovakia
and the new Austria, without reference to German or Russian views or power.

It is clear that such a picture is divorced from
reality. If Germany is reduced to impotence at
all resembling that of 1918, it will be at the cost
of immense exhaustion also on our side. But the
one power which will not have suffered from this
process of exhaustion will be Russia. And to assume that the frontiers and general position of
Poland, or of Balkan or Baltic States, or the future
of the Far East in respect of China, and our rela-

tions with Japan, can be settled without reference
to Russia, whom we can continue to treat as a
sort of unclean outlaw, indicates on our part a
disinclination to face unpleasant facts as great as
that which rendered our victory futile in 1918.

It is a common experience that facts which we
refuse to face because they have the appearance
of being unpleasant, cease to be as unpleasant
as they looked, when faced and tackled coura-
geously; can often indeed be turned to advantage.
I suggest it is so in this case.

How should we meet the situation of stalemate
just indicated, if it should prove that the cost of
breaking the stalemate is too great?

If it would be folly to attempt to end stalemate
by frontal attack upon lines which would leave
us utterly exhausted at the end, it would, for all
the reasons indicated in the preceding pages, be
almost worse folly to end it by surrender. The
fact that we may not be able to secure a military
decision in the older sense, is no argument for
submission, for the cessation of resistance. For
that *would* immediately ensure a military decision
—in favour of Germany.

Mr. G. B. Shaw suggests that we can now very
well make peace on the basis of the present situation since Russia has stopped Hitler's advance in
the East; that if we fear Hitler's domination of

Europe we can afford to wait until he tries it, and then resist him in company with Russia; and that if we fear world domination by Germany, wait until she tries it and then resist in company with the United States.

Hitler will never attempt "the domination of Europe" or "world domination" as a proclaimed purpose. It is not his method. When he reoccupied the Rhineland he was not proceeding to dominate Europe, but to reoccupy his own territory. When he annexed Austria he was not "dominating Europe," but incorporating a German people—whence he himself came—into the greater Reich. The absorption of Sudetenland was not "dominating Europe." It was, again, absorbing a German population into the Reich. When the protectorate of Bohemia was proclaimed he was not "dominating Europe," but taking obvious measures for the protection of the frontiers of the Reich. Slovakia *idem.* In demanding the return to the Reich of Danzig and German-inhabited territories in Poland he was not "dominating Europe." He was asserting the right of German people to live in one Reich with one folk under one Führer. No single step constitutes "the domination of Europe," and if we are to separate each from what goes before, and what is likely to follow, there will be no resistance justified on the

ground of "defending Europe"—as Hitler has so
well and so strikingly himself explained in *Mein
Kampf*.

No single one of the acts just enumerated can
ever be isolated as of itself constituting "a threat
to Europe." But nevertheless the sum of them,
and the development of the policy which under-
lies them, can only end in the domination of
Europe.

To wait until the aggression "threatens the
domination of the world" will be to wait until it
is too late to resist it, for by that time the forces
necessary to resistance will have been undermined
or destroyed.

Without resistance to Germany not only can
there be no international society of any kind, but
there can be no partnership with her. If we say
to Germany: "We invite you to be partners, to
share our Empire on a basis of equality, but if
you insist on being our masters instead of our
partners, on owning and governing our Empire,
instead of sharing it with us, then we shall not
resist your will"—to say that makes even partnership with Germany impossible. Our first task is
resistance to domination.

It is, of course, true—and this is perhaps the
most vital truth of all—that domination of ourselves by Germany would, in the event of our

victory over her, merely be followed by domination of Germany by us, unless we recognize that
what we are fighting for is a principle, rule, law,
by which (*a*) we ourselves are prepared to abide,
and (*b*) offer to Germany.

How can the necessary resistance to Germany
be achieved in view of the military situation just
outlined?

It is here suggested that stalemate, if properly
used by us, can be made to mean the defeat of
Hitler and victory for us.

Before considering how that can be done, it is
worth noting that if we did achieve the complete
collapse of both Russia and Germany, we should
then face immense dangers of falling into the very
same traps into which we fell in 1919—an exas-
perated public opinion particularly in France,
demanding the break-up of Germany; an exas-
perated bourgeois and reactionary Right demanding the "end of Bolshevism"; a peace, that is,
which would defy and try to bottle up all the
forces of German nationalism, exacerbated by yet
another defeat, and all the forces of working-class
discontent rendered more bitter and more profound from a sense of having been betrayed by
those who had professed to stand for freedom and
for welfare. That would indeed make certain a
future of chaos and dark night, of retaliatory vio-

lences and ferocities beyond imagination. There
is a better way.

§

Let us take stock of certain things already
achieved.

We entered this war to "stop Germany." She
has been stopped—by Russia. All those plans of
vast expansion which make up so much of the
Nazi platform and the Nazi Bible, the "*lebensraum*" which was to be found in the break-up of
Russia, in the rich wheatfields of the Ukraine; the
expansion into the Baltic areas, the definite acquisition of the lands opened up five centuries ago by
the Teutonic knights, where rich and prosperous
German colonies have already been established;
the expansion to the North East, to the South
East, towards the Black Sea and the lands of the
East and Far East—all that has been surrendered
and surrendered, moreover, to a Power which
Hitler had declared to be the supreme enemy of
Germany, and of the Nazi idea; to a Power, co-
operation with which, Hitler had written in in-
delible black and white so many times, would
mean the end of Germany.

That is capitulation indeed. How complete the
capitulation, the withdrawal, the retreat, the rout,
in that area at least, is indicated by certain significant details. The German colonies established

for five hundred years in the Baltic area covered by Lithuania, Latvia and Esthonia, immeasurably more important both economically and politically, and in terms of the German future than those in Africa, have been surrendered to Stalin, under a form of surrender much more drastic than anything imposed by the Treaty of Versailles. The colonists, sometimes at forty-eight hours' notice, have had to leave their homes, possessions, everything; their ancient estates, hallowed by family memories and centuries of labour, all this they have had to abandon from one day to another. Hitler has imposed upon German nationals and colonists terms of a material and spiritual severity, involving bitterness and humiliation, which could not have been worse if imposed by a completely victorious conqueror upon a completely defeated enemy.

That indicates the degree of the check, the defeat, the frustration of Hitler's power in areas which had been earmarked for German expansion.

But, it may be argued, just because her expansion East and South East has been checked, Germany is likely to attempt with greater energy to find compensatory outlet elsewhere.

Can we use the stalemate already produced to check Hitler's advance in the West, as effectively as Stalin has used Russia's neutrality to frustrate Hitler's advance in the East?

The answer to that question is very simple. Undoubtedly Hitler's advance can be brought to a stop, and his whole scheme of domination frustrated, provided that the West can unify itself so as to act as a defensive whole. If no such unification is possible, if Hitler and, or, Stalin can pick off one lesser State after another, without any resistance by the remainder, dividing the spoils between the conquerors, then clearly the West can be destroyed in detail, and Germany and Russia will have triumphed.

Furthermore, if France and Britain did manage, despite Western disunity, to secure victory as in 1918, and by virtue of it to restore Poland and Czecho-Slovakia, that restoration would be as impermanent after the next victory as it has proved to be after the last, if the same policy follows.

Let us note the situation, assuming that the air convention already referred to is maintained.

The British and French domination of the sea —the North Sea, the Atlantic, the Mediterranean, will not be less complete as the war goes on. It is likely to be more complete. It will enable both Britain and France to call upon and mobilize, first of all the resources of their own respective empires, the foodstuffs, the raw materials necessary for the maintenance of sea domination, and of sufficient air power to ensure that the air stalemate shall not be broken. This means that the sources of material power will include nearly the whole world outside Germany: the whole of Africa, including South Africa, Egypt, Algeria, Tunis; India, Indo-China, the West Indies, the Pacific Islands; Australia, New Zealand, Canada, South America, and, of most immediate importance of all, the inexhaustible arsenal of the United States. The Allies will be able to draw upon all that, and forbid those resources to the enemy. In the long run—and not a very long run at that—it is clear that these resources will far more than counterbalance any aid which Russia may be able to give to Germany. Russian resources are indeed far less accessible to Germany than overseas resources are to Britain. The sea road is ever ready for the ships which we can build, to a degree which railroads, not yet built in Russia, are not available for providing Germany with Russian resources, potentially vast it is true, but actually unavailable.

But in what way can the resources be used in order to prevent the achievement of Hitlerite domination? If the stalemate continues they will not be used mainly in battle, as before in the slaughter matches of the Great War, with their casualties running into millions.

Nevertheless these resources may be mobilized in such a way as to ensure the undermining of nearly everything upon which the power of Hitler has been built, its psychological, spiritual and material foundations.

Already the long series of cheap Hitlerian victories has stopped. There are no more victories, but instead, as we have seen, retreats, surrenders, surrender to the chiefest enemy of all. Yet, continued victory, as some of the preceding pages have shown, was the very condition of Hitler's command over the emotions of his people; the much promised "*lebensraum*," expansion, of Germany is not being fulfilled. The reign of plenty which was to proceed therefrom is receding, and is being replaced by ever-tightening hardship, scarcity, penury.

It is quite clear that if that situation can be maintained long enough, profound disillusion awaits the German people. That "dynamism" which is the very heart, as Dr. Rauschning has explained, of the Nazi success, the very life of the Nazi order, will begin to work against a Hitler who has become impotent and who surrenders to proclaimed enemies. The restless young men, the sorely tried small bourgeois, to say nothing of the mass of the workers, hypnotized heretofore by Hitler's success, and supporting him in foreign ventures, will begin to find the only outlet for their activity, for the dynamism, in some movement against Hitler, against the regime. And that,

indeed, is already beginning. It will be for us to
see that the circumstances do not become such as
to turn the new movement against Nazism into a
movement for an equally totalitarian Bolshevism.

But to deprive Hitler of his hypnotic dynamism
is only the negative half of the policy which we
must follow. Continued resistance is indispensable, but of itself it will not achieve our ends.
To the German, disillusioned of the Hitlerite conquering myth, of the promises of ever expanding
power, glory, prosperity, must be submitted also
the picture of an alternative means of *"lebensraum,"* expansion, prosperity, welfare.

§

Implicit in much that has been written in the
foregoing pages is the fact that one of our major
difficulties will be to persuade the enemy people
and the neutrals that this time we mean what we
say when we speak of fighting for principles of
security and equality of right as important to the
world as a whole as to ourselves.

There is one means by which we can prove that
we mean business; by beginning to put our
vaguely outlined plans into execution *now*.

There are two immediate steps which more
than anything else whatsoever would show
whether and to what degree we ourselves are
prepared for the unification of the West, are ready

for the Federal idea; which would tend to convince the world—neutral and enemy peoples alike —of the reality of our professions about a new international system. And that is to begin, now, to build up a real federal unity with France; to make of the French and British Empires a unit, not merely for war purposes, but as the beginning of the permanent reconstruction of Europe and the world along new lines. Concurrently a persistent drive should be made towards a real Federal Union of the Commonwealth. We should begin to accustom ourselves and the world to think of France and Britain, not as two countries of about forty million people each (confronted by a greater Germany twice the size of either), but as a single country of eighty millions, the pivot of a union of an additional five hundred millions, girdling the world.

The beginning of some kind of Franco-British federalism might be found in the Franco-British Supreme Council already linked with Franco-British Boards for Shipping, Purchase of Supplies, Exchange Problems. There might well be established, by private effort at first, a Franco-British Interparliamentary Conference, first of all between like-minded parties of both parliaments, going on to conferences of representatives of all British and all French parties.

The essence of any plan for "federalizing defence" should be its operation *in peace time* as well as in war.

The other day a Canadian commentator noted that although the Dominion publics for years had been insisting that they would not be dragged into Britain's Continental entanglements, here they were joining in a war which had arisen out of a line of policy that they had no part in determining. Furthermore, if Britain in the future were to stand for the defence of France, she must have some part in determining the policy out of which the necessity for defence might arise.

In other words, if there is to be co-operation in war, there must be a common foreign policy— British, French, Dominion—in peace; otherwise we do in fact place our fate, in Sir John Simon's words, in the hands of foreign governments, who may force us into war.

Nor is that all.

If to-day, Denmark, or Holland were faced with a German invasion, they would be overwhelmed, as Poland was overwhelmed. Their resources for defence would not be equal to standing up to German power. But if Britain, Finland, Norway, Sweden, Denmark, Holland, Belgium, France, Italy were one country, such a country obviously would not be powerless to resist Germany. It would in fact be impregnable, for its resources would be so distributed, and defensive arrangements so made, as to be able to meet either German or Russian power. In other words, if defence is to be effective, it must mean that defensive arrangements—military and naval budgets, the distribution of resources—must be co-ordinated in peace time. That is what is meant in this book by the term "federalism for defence."

Such military and naval federalism could not operate, of course, without a great deal of economic federalism. In order to achieve that there should be added another step, already referred to in the preceding pages. To the democracies of the Atlantic seaboard and Scandinavia we should say: "We are prepared to regard you economically as part of the Commonwealth, if you so desire. If you think there is any advantage in the 'possession' of empire, come in and share the possession. You, Denmark, can, if you will, occupy the same position economically as Canada or Australia; can participate in all Imperial Conferences for economic purposes."

It is the position which they would occupy in any Federal system; but it could be offered them *now*, as a step to that end, and as proof that we mean business.

From our point of view, why not? If a Dominion like Canada or Australia is an advantage economically, it must be an advantage to add similar "Dominions." From the point of view of those envious of our imperial possessions, the way to dispel the envy would be precisely such an offer to "own" the Empire with us.

There is something else. The dominant note of German propaganda as we have seen is that Britain has made herself rich and the rest of the world poor by stealing a quarter of the earth, thus depriving other nations of necessary "living space"; a picture of a bloated John Bull living richly and easily, while others starve as the result of a grossly inequitable division of the world's wealth.

The argument that no one is taken in by such words as "ownership," nor by that picture, has been shown in the preceding pages to be untrue. It has been shown that even Americans—in books, in editorials, on platforms—keep on saying, "There can be no peace in the world so long as one small island off the north-west coast of Europe owns a quarter of the earth. The Have-Nots of the earth will never stand it, and ought not to." Nothing could so quickly dispel this misconception as to say to the world: "If you really believe we Dominions, Canada, Britain, Australia, own our Empire, come in and own it with us. Be, economically, one of the Dominions."

There is a further point in relation to making the Federal idea a reality by beginning to apply it now. If the German people saw that it was being applied, that it had a future, that States brought within its scope gained thereby political and economic advantage, were placed on a plane of complete equality with the great empires, having unhampered access to their markets and their raw materials, then the division of Germany into several states, which the French may demand, would lose much of its terror.

Already some of those in France who voice the slogan, *"il faut en finir,"* are demanding a separate Rhineland State, a detached Bavaria. That way lies disaster, *unless* the separated German States join a union on honestly equal terms with ourselves, and the union is open on those terms to other German States. The Federal principle, imaginatively and consistently applied, might make even the policy of "breaking up Germany" a step to peace instead of to another war in the next generation.

In other words, we should use the security provided by the French Maginot Line and British sea power to bring about the unification which would frustrate the ambitions of Hitler, and render them unnecessary and unattractive to the German people.

But it all depends upon some degree of popular understanding at the time of the peace making. If there is to be that, then that understanding must make some progress, while the war is going on. We failed before because as the war went on passion took charge of the public mind, swamping reason and common sense. These were blown away in gales of belligerent emotion. There had been no adequate educational preparation for the peace. We did not see why the policies for which we then clamoured—the policy of a Carthaginian Peace, of crushing Germany, of refusing to discuss the terms, of guilt clauses, of absurd Reparation claims—were foolish, any more than we saw later why we had to defend troublesome little States against aggression as the condition of our own security. The thing was not clear to us at all, and because we were confused and muddle-headed, we were fruitful soil for emotional exploitation by demagogues.

We must learn to "see why," most particularly to see the fundamental issue at the root of it all, namely, that our power must be pledged to the constitution, to the law against violence.

To achieve this establishment of law was our professed aim in the last war, stated vaguely, but repeatedly by Asquith, and with very great clarity by President Wilson. It was put forward by the latter as the reason for America's entrance into the war. His crusade received the widest possible support in the United States. A "League to Enforce Peace" was supported by both the great American parties. The argument "if a nation in future attempts aggression, it will find itself confronted by forces that cannot be overcome, will learn that 'aggression does not pay,' " was an argument which excited the greatest popular enthusiasm.

Yet because that enthusiasm did not imply real understanding of what the method involved, the whole scheme was tragically short-lived. Though it is clear that if power is to have deterrent effect, the potential aggressor must be able to foresee that his aggression will indeed meet the collective power envisaged in the method, there was soon flat refusal on the part of the enthusiasts to fulfil this necessary part of the plan. For it meant commitment beforehand; and immediately the enthusiastic supporters of the scheme saw that it involved a pledge to defend the victim of violence, they saw also that it meant "foreign entanglements," in disregard of the Washingtonian counsel. It was no conscientious objection to arms as such which stood in the way. It was the belief that arms could be used most effectively for defence if each nation defended himself, and all refused to defend the law.

But this, of course, is precisely what a potential aggressor intent upon expansion would desire. If his expansion could be piece-meal, tackling first one nation while the others remained quiescent, then another while the remainder were equally

quiescent, of course there could never be effective
resistance to aggression at all. The American plan
was quickly dropped by its most enthusiastic
American supporters because those supporters had
realized neither its implications nor indeed adequately realized its need, realized, that is, that
their own defence would depend upon some common defence or law.

The plan was rejected equally both in Britain
and in France by a combination of most disparate
forces. It was rejected by the Pacifist because it
involved the use of force; by the militarist because it involved internationalism; by the Isolationist because it involved commitment; by the
Imperialist because our business was to defend
the Empire, not foreigners; by the Socialist because "the cause of war is Capitalism, and the
only way to get rid of war is to destroy Capitalism"; by the Capitalist because the risk of war
with Japan, or Italy, or Germany was temporarily
disturbing to financial security, investment and
trade; by the Liberal because liberalism was his-
torically hostile to "entangling alliances"; by the
Conservative because it put foreign policy in the
hands of a lot of foreign governments; by the low-
brow because we ought to mind our own business
and not go interfering with a lot of Czechs, or
Abyssinians, or Manchurians, or Chinese, or
Japanese, or Italians, or other outlandish folk; by

the highbrow because you could never get common action so long as national sovereignty was preserved; by the unimaginative who felt that the League of Nations was a dream; by the imaginative because the League of Nations was not a world state or a world federation; by the uneducated with an Oxford accent because collective action against aggression "tended to make every local quarrel a world quarrel," and because if we had asserted the principle of collective defence we should, it was argued with complete fallacy, have had war with Japan, war with Italy, war with Germany, and so bargains with the aggressor seemed preferable; by the uneducated with an 'Oxton accent because matters of employment, wages, prices were more important than the fate of Poles and Czechs; and by all these categories because they all alike failed to balance the foregoing considerations against other considerations that should have been taken into account.

So we have made the worst of both worlds. If repression of Germany had been carried out thoroughly, and her attempts at rearmament jumped on, with energy, we should not be in the present position. If we had made the most of the opposite policy of conciliation in the early stages, had nursed the Weimar Republic with every consideration, brought it at once into the League on a basis of absolute equality, dropped Reparations, we should not now be in this present position. We followed neither road consistently. Conciliation was defeated by the maintenance of the blockade after the war; by such features as insistence upon the war guilt clause; by the maintenance of absurd Reparations clauses; by our own refusal to disarm. Having then created the maximum of resentment, we thereupon refused to act co-operatively to restrain its effects.

The degree of ignorance and bad political judgment which defeated the League would also have defeated Federal Union, which does not ask less departure from the familiar, less sacrifice of vested interest and prejudice, but more. There would have been more for the public to become confused about, more fallacious arguments to invoke, more misapprehension to overcome.

To avoid a repetition of it all, we must do our best, this time, to put first things first. A long period of "White War" may help us.

It is not an accident that those who made the American Union, whose example we in Europe are so repeatedly urged to follow, had during years of warfare learned the need, as one of the signers of the Declaration of Independence put it, of hanging together as the only alternative to hanging separately. They were taught unity not merely by war, but by the strength of the power which after war still faced them; which had in no sense collapsed, and with which, indeed, a generation later, they were to be once more at war. The literature of the American federal effort reveals how vivid was this sense that the price of security was unity.

We have to apply that truth in different and more difficult conditions, a truth obscured by complexities which the learned have tended to make still more obscure.

Had the political task of American federation been crossed by conflicts of the kind which the protagonists of the class war, among others, en- visage; if powerful sections in the colonies had had constantly advanced some argument equiva- lent to that we hear so often now, that the road to peace is not Federalism, but Socialism ("you must get rid of Capitalism"); then there would have been no American Union, and we should have had wars between the independent republics of New York and New Jersey, Pennsylvania and Ohio, as we have had wars between the inde- pendent republics of Chile and Peru, Bolivia and Paraguay. Because the political problem was tackled first, and tackled successfully; because the need of political unity for self-preservation was very consciously present in the minds of those who worked for federation, it succeeded and there has been peace between the states of the Amer- ican Union, a peace due not to the abolition of

Capitalism, or any similar economic process, but to a political factor. Having achieved it the economic problem has not been rendered more difficult than in those other American republics which did not become welded into similar large Federations. The absence of wars on the North American continent, and the absence of national barriers have rendered many aspects of the economic problem that much the easier to solve. The problem that faces Europe is first of all a political one. Its solution will make solution of the economic problem that much easier.

There are many ways in which we in Europe may achieve our necessary unity. The way is less important than the will. And the will depends upon the plain man seeing clearly the need for this one foundation to the house of Europe and mankind. Truly the foundation is not the house; but without such foundation no house can stand, and shelter us from the storms which threaten us with such misery and torment.